THE
PROBLEMS
DO NOT LIE
IN YOUR
Thighs

A JOURNEY OF HEALING, SELF-LOVE,
AND RECLAIMING MY POWER

BECKIE KULLBERG

The Problems Do Not Lie in Your Thighs
A Journey of Healing, Self-Love, and Reclaiming My Power

Best Life Journey
Beckiekullberg.com
Cotati, CA

Book Design by Transcendent Publishing | TranscendentPublishing.com
Cover photo credit: Grace Brooke
Edited by Mary Rembert

ISBN: 979-8-218-56817-7

This book is a work of nonfiction. The experiences, views, and opinions expressed within this book are the author's own and are shared to inspire and provide insights based on personal experience. Any resemblance to real persons, living or dead, or real-life events is purely coincidental. The author does not provide professional mental health advice and encourages readers to seek qualified professionals if needed.

Printed in the United States of America.

"I love and approve of myself, therefore I am worthy of all good that comes to me."
—Louise L. Hay

CONTENTS

DEDICATION

This book is dedicated to all the women out there who have settled for less, loathed their bodies, or didn't accept an invitation to a party because they didn't know what to wear. It's time to take back your life and take back your body!

ACKNOWLEDGMENTS

*T*hank you to those who have truly supported me in my life and endeavors. Having a supportive circle is crucial for success. As a strong, independent woman, I am proud to say that I have not done it alone.

My number one fan is my husband. He is always behind me with all my crazy ideas, supporting and cheering me on.

My son inspires me every single day to do and be better. His courage and tenacity are just a couple of his best traits.

Debbie spends hours listening to me talk about my dreams and cheering me on for every single one. She's honest with me, and I trust her.

Angie, my friend since junior high school, inspires me to live a life of excellence and holds me capable beyond what I see for myself.

Mindy for being my biggest cheerleader.

Shelly, I am so glad I picked up on you in Hollywood.

Marie, thank you for always making me laugh. We will always have The Rental Place down the road.

Elizabeth, aka E. You complete me!

My newest friend, Mariah, who reminds me we are not average!

INTRODUCTION

*I*t's time to put an end to the idea that your problems lie in your thighs, arms, belly, butt, or any other body part for that matter. For far too long, we've been sold the idea that our appearance is the key to success, happiness, and fulfillment. The truth is that our bodies are just one aspect of who we are. We are complex, multifaceted beings with a lot more to offer than just a pretty face, a toned body, or perfect morning hair.

We are all unique in our appearance and gifts. This is to be celebrated, not discouraged. Strive to stand out, not fit in.

I used to believe, "If only my thighs were perfect, my arms weren't flabby, my stomach was flat, my butt was smaller or bigger, blah, blah, blah … my life would be perfect." This belief was always running in the background of my mind. Whether I was conscious of it or not, it was there.

I am here to tell you I fell into that trap for years and wasted so much time and energy believing all of it was true. Now, in my journey of self-discovery and coaching, I realize that it is all a big fat lie! Yes, I said it, A BIG FAT LIE! At some point in our lives, we get fed this BS and believe and buy into that lie. It's not true and never was true. Right now, in this very moment, you get to decide if you want to keep telling yourself this story OR if you are ready, and I mean really ready, for a new story.

If you choose to write a new story of who you are and what makes you special and unique, write a good one, Best Seller quality.

In this book, I will explore the reasons behind our obsession with our physical appearance and how it's holding us back from living our best lives, the lives we were meant to live. I'll also share my journey to body acceptance and that moment when I realized I was no longer ashamed of my body.

I will share all of that and my story of how I got to a place of loving the woman I see in the mirror and having an incredible partner in life to share all of my success.

At the end of each chapter, I will ask you three questions so you can go deeper on that topic. You may want to start a journal as you reflect on them.

This is the book I wish I had as a teenager, and I suggest you get one for every woman you know. It's time for a revolution! Wait, it's time for a coming together of the thighs, all the great thighs.

Chapter 1

YOU WOULD BE SO MUCH BETTER AT SEX IF ONLY ...

"You would be so much better at sex if your thighs weren't so big," I heard him say. The shame and embarrassment burned on my face, and as I sat there, partially clothed, I wanted to shrink or disappear. I couldn't look at him, nor could I say a word. I was frozen, paralyzed. All I could think of was that my worth and desirability hinged on the size of my body, specifically my thighs.

His words stung hard, and he had absolutely no clue. I guess he believed he was doing me a favor by telling me this. Maybe this was pity sex for him.

He wasn't the first to say something like that, and he wasn't the last.

It felt like I could only be loved if I shrunk myself. This gnawed at me, especially since this was the first time I had explored being on top during sex.

When I went home that night, I lay in bed and cried silently so my parents wouldn't hear me. I never saw or heard from whatever his name was again.

I told myself I would never put myself in that position again. I lied.

I was 16 and wanted to feel lovable, pretty, and wanted. I wanted to wake up looking like those models on the cover of *Cosmopolitan* magazine who looked like they didn't have a care in the world and were always deemed lovable and beautiful by the opposite sex.

Why did boys only want one thing and never look back as if I were yesterday's leftovers?

Why did I keep falling for it?

I'd show them! I'll lose weight and then flaunt my hot body toward them, and when they make a pass at me, I will resist and let them know they don't get me again.

*   *   *

I grew up in a small town in California called Chico, and it was always super hot in the summer, so swimming and tubing down the Sacramento River was a big part of our lives.

Up until puberty, my body appeared emaciated. My stomach was concave, and I never paid any attention to how I looked. I never minded wearing shorts or a swimsuit. Post puberty, my breasts grew seemingly overnight, my thighs filled out, and not in a good way, and my arms were bigger than my friends.

Because of the way my body filled out, my mom thought it would be a good idea to put me on a diet at 13 years old. She had been going to The Diet Center, and a few years prior, she had lost about 100 pounds. Even though she was on the road to gaining it back, she saw The Diet Center as a place to successfully lose weight.

I didn't think I needed to go on a diet; I wanted to please my mom.

We would get in the car every morning before school, and she and I would go to The Diet Center and weigh in. I remember walking in either feeling elated because the day before I was "on plan" OR it was the walk of shame because I cheated and knew that scale never lied.

This was when I was in junior high. Junior freaking high school! The time when your hormones are all over the place, and you don't know why.

If my weight was down, it would be a great day. I would get out of the car at drop-off and float to my first class with all the confidence in the world while I was getting closer to my goal weight and dreaming of those tiny jeans I so wanted to wear like the skinny girls. In the early eighties, the popular jeans were Chemin de Fer and Ditto, and they were not made for girls with curves; they were designed for skinny girls.

If my weight was up at weigh-in, I would be an emotional wreck! At school drop-off, I felt like a complete and total loser as I mentally beat myself up for eating a Ritz cracker the day before, or maybe I ate "on plan" and was convinced that my body wanted to hold weight because I was meant to be fat and ugly. When I walked into class, I would hold back the tears that threatened to roll down my face and scream out to all of Chico Junior High that I had gained two pounds, and in my mind, it was obvious!

When I was going to The Diet Center, I weighed around 130 pounds, and at 5' 2" (that's a stretch, closer to 5' 1¾"), I was considered overweight.

Although I don't remember exactly what I weighed when I started or what my goal weight was then, the daily weigh-ins still burn in my memory as a shameful and hellish experience.

For the record, I don't harbor any ill feelings toward The Diet Center and believe they were genuinely helping people. This was the era of low-fat dieting.

My mom didn't want me to turn out just like her, so taking me to The Diet Center was her way of saying I love you. My mom was obese most of her adult life. She gained and lost 100 pounds several times.

That diet was the start of an eating disorder called binge eating disorder (BED) that I would battle and overcome in my forties. When I was diagnosed with BED, I had no idea such a thing existed. I just thought I was lazy and had no willpower over food.

Over the years, my weight has been up, and it's been down, just like my self-esteem.

If I could talk to 13-year-old Beckie, I would tell her she's beautiful, lovable, and above all, WORTHY! Those were the words I needed to hear from my mom back then. Do I blame my mom for putting me on a diet at 13? I would love to say no, and that would be a lie. Where I find peace in all of this is that she did the best she could with the tools she had. She passed in 2020, and we had a decent relationship.

When we were going to The Diet Center together, she said, "I don't want you to turn out like me." By that, she meant overweight, obsessed with food, and miserable. My guess is the reason we had only a decent relationship is that, in many ways, I did turn out just like her with my relationship with food and my body.

We live in a culture that worships physical beauty and equates it with success, happiness, and being sexy. From magazines to movies, billboards to social media, we're bombarded with images of perfect bodies and flawless faces. We're taught that if we can just achieve this level of physical perfection, we'll be happy, successful, and fulfilled.

I see this shifting in the media, and it is progress. There is an anti-diet movement that comes with its own pros and cons.

The truth is that physical perfection is an impossible standard. Our bodies are unique and constantly changing. There is no one-size-fits-all when it comes to beauty. And even if we did achieve this mythical perfection, it wouldn't guarantee us happiness or success.

I remember the moment this truly resonated for me. You might think it was after I saw a video of how much photoshopping goes into the magazine model photos—no. Or after seeing people in real life who use a filter on social media and notice they do not look the same—nope. Or maybe it was when I was treated for an eating disorder and saw how all the thin women viewed themselves as fat—nope, not that either.

One day, I looked at my body, like really looked at it, and took time to appreciate each part. Not only the parts I liked but the other parts too. The parts that I would hide with longer shorts or sleeves. The song from *The Greatest Showman* comes to mind, "This Is Me." It was truly a "This Is Me" moment. This is the body that God gave me, and who am I to say or think it is less than beautiful?

Did this moment make me instantly love every inch of my body? No. It did start the journey of acceptance. Forgiveness. Eventually, love.

This is what I wish for you.

If you are in the space of believing that your life will suddenly be perfect when you're at a certain weight or your thighs are smaller, then keep reading ... my Greatest Showman moment didn't happen until my forties ... and it happened. Once I had and felt forgiveness and love for my body, I could not go back, EVER!

My intention with this book is to help you see your body as beautiful, embrace your perceived flaws, and love the person you see in the mirror. It's time!

You may wonder if there are days when I less than love what I see in the mirror or in photos, and the answer is yes, absolutely. It's like a bad hair day. Here's the difference. I don't beat myself up for it. My thighs have more cellulite on them this week. It's a notice, not a wrecking ball. Then, it's a choice for me on what I want to do with this information. Do I want to tell myself I am ugly, worthless, or unlovable? Or do I want to tell myself I chose to eat more and move less the last week or more ...? I get to choose, and so do you.

It really is a choice. The perception we have of ourselves is a choice.

Physical perfection DOES NOT EXIST! Read that last sentence again. When I had my "This Is Me" moment, my mind was blown, and that belief that I needed to have a perfect body to be lovable blew out of my mind like dust on a dirt road. This shift can be quick or more subtle over time until one day, you catch your reflection in a storefront window and like it. Be open to it. It might not look like mine or anyone else's; it will be unique to you.

The way I see it, we have one chance in this life, and we either get to suffer through loathing our bodies or learn to love what God gave us. Every moment of every day, you can choose how you feel and think about your body.

REFLECTIVE QUESTIONS

1. What are some of the beliefs you have about physical appearance and its connection to success, happiness, and fulfillment?
2. How have these beliefs affected your life and self-esteem?
3. What would your life look like if you weren't so focused on physical appearance?

Chapter 2

THE REAL REASONS
WE FOCUS ON OUR APPEARANCE

So why do we put so much emphasis on our physical appearance? Why do we, mostly women, put our worth in our appearance? More importantly, why do we continue to do this even though we now know more than ever that we are more than what we look like?

Here are a few reasons:

Social Conditioning: We've been conditioned by society to believe that our appearance is the most important thing about us. We're taught that we'll be judged and valued based on our looks, and our worth is tied to our physical appearance. This isn't necessarily blatantly taught.

This seems to be most common in women. I don't make the rules; this book would not be needed if I did because we would all love ourselves as perfectly imperfect.

Insecurity: Many of us struggle with feelings of insecurity and self-doubt. We believe that if we can just fix our appearance, we'll feel better about ourselves, be more confident, and overall happier.

Insert the diet industry! More on that later.

Control: Focusing on our appearance gives us a sense of control. We believe that if we can control our bodies, we can control our lives. This control comes from how we eat, what we weigh, and/or what we wear.

Let's break down these three areas.

SOCIAL CONDITIONING

Social conditioning is the sociological process of training individuals in a society to act or respond in a manner generally approved by society and peer groups within society. That's a lot of jargon, meaning we just want to fit in and be accepted.

This one seems obvious, especially in an era with social media dominating our lives. Yet this goes back long before Instagram, Facebook, and even the car were ever invented.

This conditioning starts when we are very little and learn how to act and behave in a socially acceptable manner. Throwing toys at your sister is not acceptable; instead, I guess handing the toy to her is. Maybe she deserved it? Putting gum in your brother's hair is not acceptable. Sorry about that, Jason. Handing him an unwrapped piece of gum is the more acceptable choice.

You see, getting along with others is all about social conditioning and what's acceptable and not acceptable. We learn from our parents, at school, and through shows we watch as to what is deemed appropriate behavior in public and even not in public.

We, as humans, act in a certain way and, in turn, get a positive response; we like that and want to keep doing what we just did. For example, when I lost weight in high school, the boys started noticing me more. Even the really cute, popular guys started talking to me. The social conditioning here is to lose weight and be thin to get guys to go out with you or talk to you in history class.

We do something and get a positive response, so we keep doing it and more of it.

In this era, we post a photo laced with filters erasing fine lines, narrowing our faces, and giving us a more vibrant look, and our friends "like" and comment on how great our skin looks. "What have you been doing"? "Wow, you never seem to age," or "You look just like you did 20 years ago."

Insert rant: just like party hats, filters are meant for fun, not an everyday and every photo occurrence. I am going to say this once— stop using filters. Please stop using filters! In my personal opinion, I believe using filters all the time says you don't believe you are pretty enough without them. Also, others compare themselves to a look that is not possible.

As I write this book, TikTok has a filter called "Bold Glamour," and it makes almost every person look like they have flawless skin, perfectly applied makeup, and the shape of their face is perfect. Have I tried it, you ask? Absolutely! Did I record and share a video using said filter—absolutely! It was a one-time deal to test for FUN.

Have you ever only seen a person with filters and then met them in person and realized, yikes, they have wrinkles and sagging skin? It's not fun to stare at someone and wonder, "What the heck!?" My face cannot lie, and it didn't that day either. I was shocked!

Truth bomb here: yes, we, including myself, look at people and judge them on their appearance. If you say you don't, ahem, let's be honest, okay? We do. I do. My theory on this goes back to caveman days and how they all judged one another as to who could hunt best, bear children, and protect the tribe from harm. It was all about survival, and we still have that natural urge to judge in us.

There's nothing wrong with judging people on their looks. It's what you do with that judgment that matters. If you treat someone poorly or disrespectfully because they don't look the way you think they should look, well, that's just wrong, and you're a jerk.

Social conditioning is when we believe the most important thing about us is how we look and that our worth is tied to our physical appearance. This book is meant to shift that focus to go deeper into what you see in others and how you show yourself to others …

Usually, the flaws you notice in someone else can be linked back to your own flaws. As long as I can remember, I have been self-conscious about my arms, therefore I have noticed other people's arms. And by notice, I mean sometimes I compare, thinking, *Oh, her arms are bigger than mine. She is so brave to bare her arms. Why can't I feel comfortable in a sleeveless top like she does?* OR *Wow, she has GREAT arms; I wish mine looked like hers.*

INSECURITY

Insecurity is an uncertainty or anxiety about oneself, a lack of confidence.

Everyone feels insecure about something at some time in their lives. It's a natural feeling on occasion. However, we are not meant to stay there.

Do I ever feel insecure about my body? Yes. There are days when I look at my legs or see a photo of myself and think, ugh, why do I have so much cellulite? This used to trip me up, and I would not just see the cellulite; I'd then focus on my crow's feet, the sagging skin on my arms, and anything else I could find wrong with myself. It was like once I saw one thing I didn't like, I could find a hundred.

The reverse works too … when I see one thing about my body I love, I can find a hundred more.

Insecurity breeds more insecurity, and confidence breeds more confidence. What you focus on grows. When I am most insecure about my body, it's typically when other things in my life aren't working out as I planned, and beating up on myself for my chubby thighs is the low-hanging fruit.

If my business is slow, it's so much easier to say, hey, if only my thighs were smaller, more people would want to work with me instead of getting out there and doing the work of getting new clients. This default deflection happens without my even noticing. No new clients; it must be my thighs. They saw that photo I posted recently, noticed my thighs, and thought they could never work with someone with thighs the size of tree trunks.

Even typing that makes me laugh, and yet, it happens so naturally that I don't even notice it until it has cycled through several times. For you, the cycle could sound different. My boss chose someone else for the position I wanted; it must be because my arms are flabby. This thought isn't conscious, so you don't even realize it is happening. Suddenly, the flabby arms take center stage, and you don't even think about why you didn't get the position, and that time in second grade when you were embarrassed for falling off the swings, and you go down a rabbit hole of how terrible you are. It's a cycle, and the exciting news is it can be interrupted.

I don't like to share this part of insecurity, and yet it's so important to read, know, and recognize. Some industries exploit insecurities. I choose to share this because I believe it's important to decipher whether you are buying a product because you truly want it or because its marketing has made you feel crummy about yourself, and if you use what they are selling, all of your problems will go away.

Beauty and Cosmetics

The beauty industry often thrives on making individuals feel inadequate about their natural appearance. With airbrushed models, digitally enhanced advertisements, and now AI, it perpetuates an unattainable standard of beauty that keeps consumers returning for products promising to "fix" imperfections. Hey, I love makeup just as much as most women do. What I don't like are the airbrushed models (this goes back to filters) that sell a look that cannot be obtained, no matter how much makeup you purchase.

To the woman who believes she can never leave the house without makeup, why? What do you believe will happen? If this is you, I challenge you to go out au naturel!

I used to never want to post videos on social media if my hair and makeup weren't perfect. When I felt inspired to share something, typically, it was when I was out on a walk or hike and in pigtails with no makeup. So, I would note the idea and record it later when I looked all done up.

The problem with this was I didn't feel as inspired, and the video would come out more forced than if I had filmed it when I was in the moment. Then, I decided to just go with it when I was out in nature, and guess what? More people said, "Wow, I really like what you've been posting lately; it's very authentic."

Authentic, that's EXACTLY what I had been shooting for and not hitting. Why? Because I believed it needed to look a certain way, and I needed to look a certain way to land with people. NOPE! People want, see, and love AUTHENTICITY!

Have you ever heard the saying, "People don't remember what you said; they remember the way you made them feel." Posting videos while I was feeling it gave the viewer the feeling too. One of my favorite famous people, Mel Robbins, demonstrated this as she bravely posted videos with tousled hair and no makeup.

Fashion

The fashion industry can be notorious for perpetuating unrealistic body ideals. By showcasing predominantly one body type and encouraging rapid fashion trends, it fuels the feeling of never being "in style" or "in shape" enough.

I'll be honest: no one has ever accused me of always being on trend. What I do like to do with clothes is wear items that fit and flatter my body. When miniskirts were all the rage, it seemed like I was the only one not in one; I donned my Bermuda shorts or an above-the-knee skirt because that was what I felt comfortable wearing and what I believed looked best on my body.

If you truly feel comfortable wearing the latest trend, go for it! If you're wearing it only because everyone else is and you don't like how you look in it or feel comfortable, consider something else. Yes, I realize this might not be a popular belief, and I am okay with that. Dress to make YOUR body shine!

Diet and Weight Loss

Dieting and weight loss companies frequently prey on the vulnerability of those with body image concerns. They profit from perpetuating the myth that a thinner body equals a happier and healthier life despite the potential harm of extreme dieting. This is by far the biggest offender in my eyes, and I could probably write an entire book on this subject.

According to the latest research study, "the demand of U.S. Weight Loss Market size and share was valued at approximately USD 135.7 billion in 2022 and is expected to reach USD 159.69 billion in 2023. The study expects that by 2030, it will reach around USD 305.30 billion, at a compound annual growth rate (CAGR) of about 9.7% during the forecast period 2023 to 2030."[1] Holy smokes!

---

[1] "[Latest] U.S. Weight Loss Market Size/Share Worth USD 305.30 Billion by 2030 at a 9.7% CAGR: Custom Market Insights (Analysis, Outlook, Leaders, Report, Trends, Forecast, Segmentation, Growth, Growth Rate, Value)." Yahoo! Finance, May 9, 2023. https://finance.yahoo.com/news/latest-u-weight-loss-market-170000586. html?guccounter=1&guce_referrer=aHR0cHM6Ly93d3cuZ29vZ2xlLmNvbS88&guce_referrer_sig=AQAAABjeO-1yTW1IGykVr1ZYuS951gCumaaSf7a_LKa_khY-WhzVCKhq8njki0GsChfHdVU9BsK8AnHJU-jd6-amEKYNZzYOZ-kPv1gOzxdiQzM_4M_vyA0-4m-Sv7StFy5oblFc-DlycnSo8adRttILaIvc_knsTxf0t56z8mT8dZQ1R.

About half of the adult U.S. population will have obesity and about a quarter will have severe obesity by 2030, according to a new study led by Harvard T.H. Chan School of Public Health.[2]

This doesn't add up to me. If the diet industry is worth over $135 billion and growing, and yet over half the adults in the U.S. are overweight, then what's missing?

If diets worked, why is such a large portion of our population overweight? There are many answers to this question, and again, I could write an entire book about it.

Plastic Surgery and Cosmetic Procedures

The desire for a perfect appearance drives the booming plastic surgery and cosmetic procedure industry. Advertisements often oversimplify procedures and rarely discuss potential risks, painting a picture of instant transformation. Please don't think I am against plastic surgery or cosmetic procedures because I am not. I had liposuction on my thighs when I was in my early thirties and an eye lift in my fifties, as well as Botox and some fillers. By the way, after liposuction, the fat does come back, and even more so in other areas.

Years ago, I had a friend who was dating a real schmuck, like a first-class jerk. They were getting ready to go out to dinner with friends, and she was all dressed up and ready to go. He looked at her and said, "That outfit really makes your tits look small." I believe actual smoke came out of my ears when she told me this. Within the year she had breast implants, and guess what, he paid for them! Did she see her tits as small, nope. She did it to keep him.

---

[2] Nicole Rura, "Close to Half of U.S. Population Projected to Have Obesity by 2030," Harvard T.H. Chan, April 19, 2019, https://www.hsph.harvard.edu/news/press-releases/half-of-us-to-have-obesity-by-2030/.

Now, this story isn't the fault of the plastic surgery industry, nor do I put any blame on them. The problem lies with men like that and women who believe them. This goes back to social conditioning. If a man says we look good, we like that. If he says otherwise, we figure out how to get their attention. By "we," I mean some women, and I too have been there.

If you are choosing any type of plastic surgery or cosmetic procedure, please do so because you want to do it for yourself, not anyone else. It's permanent; jerks are temporary.

The cold, hard truth is that these industries exploit insecurities because it's profitable. Insecurities are a lucrative market, and promoting unrealistic beauty standards keeps consumers hooked.

Here's why they continue to thrive on exploiting these vulnerabilities:

> **Profit Motive:** At its core, these industries are driven by profit. Insecurities create a continuous demand for products and services, leading to substantial financial gains. Let me reiterate that I am not against plastic surgery. If you choose to go under the knife, please do so from a place of responsibility and not desperation that you will be more desirable to the opposite sex if your boobs are bigger. You are the one who gets to carry them around ALL the time.

> **Cultural Pressure:** Society often equates appearance with worth, and these industries leverage this cultural pressure to their advantage. Do I need to mention filters again …

Social Comparison: Encouraging individuals to constantly compare themselves to unattainable ideals creates a cycle of dissatisfaction, prompting consumers to keep seeking products and services to bridge the gap.

Empowering Ourselves: The first step to counteract this exploitation is awareness. Recognizing that these industries thrive on insecurities empowers us to make more informed choices as consumers. We can choose to support brands and movements that celebrate diversity and promote self-acceptance, and we can prioritize self-care over self-doubt. In other words, you can vote with your money.

CONTROL

Control is an illusion. One of the compelling reasons we fixate on our appearance is the illusion of control it provides. Many of us fall into the trap of believing that if we can mold our bodies to conform to societal beauty standards, we can similarly sculpt our lives into perfection. It's the idea that by mastering our physical selves, we gain mastery over our entire existence. Read that again.

If you lean toward being a perfectionist, and so many of us with body confidence issues do, then these words sum it up for you: "If only I can get control of my body, eating, life ... then everything will be perfect." This is a never-ending cycle of working toward a target that can't be hit nor can it be obtained or even maintained.

In the pages ahead, we'll delve into strategies to break free from the grip of these industries and shift your focus toward self-love and empowerment, helping you take back control of your narrative and redefining what true beauty and success mean to you.

REFLECTIVE QUESTIONS

1. What emotions or experiences trigger your desire to change your physical appearance?

2. How has your focus on physical appearance affected your relationships and daily life?

3. What other areas of your life do you think you may be neglecting because of your focus on physical appearance?

Chapter 3

MY FIRST BINGE

While I was on the diet with my mom, I remember feeling hungry, deprived, and sorry for myself that I had to eat this way. I remember being angry that other kids were eating cinnamon rolls, Fruity Pebbles, and grilled cheese sandwiches. Meanwhile, I was eating plain chicken breasts with steamed veggies, oh yum.

The awkwardness of my teenage years, coupled with eating different foods, really set me up to be super self-conscious and compare myself to others.

I figured out that if I was losing weight, people would celebrate me, which felt good. When I was gaining weight, people gave me this look of total disappointment, which felt bad. This is where I believe I learned that I was either "good" or "bad." There was no in between. At any given moment, I was always either good or bad.

Meanwhile, my best friend, Cindy, was thin and pretty and could eat whatever she wanted. The boys loved her, and I always stood in her shadow. One day, when I got to school after weighing in and being up on the scale and crying my eyes out, Cindy asked me, "Do you really think this diet is good for you?" I was completely stunned. Did I even have a choice? No. The way I saw it was that I was fat and that is bad, and I want to be thin so I can be good.

The first time I sneaked food was a few months into the diet. I ate Ritz crackers with individually sliced cheese, and it was heaven! I would get four crackers at a time and one slice of cheese folded into quarters, and I put each quarter on a cracker. Ah, the crunch of the crackers and the creaminess of the cheese were so good!

As I ate them, I remember feeling recharged and excited. It gave me a rush. It felt wrong, and I knew I was cheating, but I was so dang hungry and sick and tired of plain old chicken breasts. I figured out how to quietly go into the pantry, get the crackers, grab the cheese, and go into my room to eat them. If I wasn't able to take them to my room, I would shove them in my mouth right there in the pantry.

The name for this behavior is closet eater—literally and figuratively. I ate in my car or when home alone and did my best to hide all the evidence.

After eating the crackers and cheese, something very strange happened: the excitement turned to this strange sense of shame, and as it filled me up inside, my thoughts turned to my mom, who would be so disappointed in me, and so would the lady at The Diet Center. Would I need to confess? The scale will be up tomorrow, and I will feel so horrible about myself. Then, when I go to school with the shame, will the other kids know what I did? Shoot, why did I do this? How could I be so stupid? How could I be so weak? What is wrong with me? I'll never do that again ...

My best guess is that's how my relationship with food and my body all started ... years of binge eating, yo-yo dieting, weight gain, weight loss, hating myself, barely liking myself, loathing myself, and making choices that kept me ashamed of myself and my body. Shame and guilt were my two best friends—not all friendships are healthy.

Through high school, my weight was up and down. I went from 160 pounds to 118 in one school year, and I remember how the boys would say, "Wow, Beckie, you look great," when I was at the lower weight. I got so much attention. I felt thin, and yet I felt fat at the same time.

I remember I had a pair of pale blue pants that fit me like a glove, and when I wore them on campus, I felt so proud of all my hard work, while at the same time, I had this sense of please don't notice me.

I hated school! The only subject I enjoyed was English. When I went into middle school, the first trimester was horrible because I didn't understand how to do what they were asking me to do. At one time, I heard my mom say they were thinking about putting me back into sixth grade so I could catch up. I went from good grades in elementary school to failing in middle school. I felt like a failure, and I was labeled a failure.

Since I did not value myself, I turned to boys to give me validation and approval. It was fitting that *Urban Cowboy* came out at that time with "Looking For Love In All The Wrong Places." That song described me perfectly!

At 14, I discovered drugs and alcohol and lost my virginity to my boyfriend Bill on his sister's living room couch after drinking

Southern Comfort. Our first time together was painful, awkward, and not at all like in the movies. When I went home that night, I wasn't sure if I should cry or celebrate. Honestly, I didn't feel like doing either.

One night, while in the back seat of his car parked at Bidwell Park, I had my first orgasm, and it was phenomenal. I had no idea my body could do that. I did not know what masturbation was and didn't know I could do that to myself until years later. Keep in mind that this was long before the internet, and my mom didn't talk to me about the birds, the bees, or the glorious things our bodies could do.

In the '80s, not a lot of moms were talking to their kids about sex and how to value their bodies; we just figured it out with a lot of mistakes along the way—speaking for myself here.

Talking about sex was not comfortable for me at all!

Drinking made me feel less self-conscious, and I really liked that. It also gave me the confidence to talk to guys where I may have been afraid while sober, and unfortunately, this led to promiscuity. I would go out with a guy for a few weeks and then on to the next very quickly.

At 16, I was carrying the shame of being promiscuous AND binge eating. When my mom found out I was no longer a virgin, she took me to our primary doctor and had him put me on the birth control pill. That was the extent of our birds and bees talk.

There was no "respect your body," "say no when you don't want to," or "wait to give it up when it's special"... nope, just a super uncomfortable silent car ride home.

One night, my best friend, her boyfriend, Dino, a friend of his, and I were driving around, and Dino dropped her off before taking me home. I didn't think anything of it until he drove toward the park instead of my house. He parked the car and forced himself on me. As I said, "No," he kept going while his friend watched from outside the car.

He wasn't fully successful, and I believe because of that his friend didn't have a go at me as he had planned. They drove me home, and as I sat in the back seat, they talked to each other as if nothing had happened.

Shortly after I got home, our phone rang, and I could hear my mom sounding concerned and angry. Then she came into my room and yelled at me, "Did you have sex with Dino?" I then got on the phone with Cindy and her mom, who was like a mother to me as I had known her my entire life, and they were both yelling at me and calling me a slut and a whore.

I was in trouble, and it all happened so fast. Just like that, I was a whore and lost my best friend. The next day at school, people talked and stared, and not one person asked my side of the story.

That memory got buried and didn't come out until 40 years later during a tapping session. That one night changed everything for me. How others saw me and how I saw myself.

NOTE: Tapping, aka EFT or emotional freedom technique, is an alternative treatment for physical pain and emotional distress. It's also referred to as psychological acupressure.

On most weekends, I would go out drinking with friends and had several one-night stands. I kept hoping sex would lead to a relationship. If I put out, then they would want to see me again. If I gave them what they wanted, they would like or even love me.

The first time I cut class I was in ninth grade. I asked a friend if she wanted to go to Orange Julius, and to my surprise, she agreed. This became a regular habit and continued into high school. The highest GPA I ever got was 1.67. There was only one way they taught: lecture followed by work. Lecture followed by work. I could never pay attention long enough to the lecture to get the material, and because I didn't get the material, I felt stupid and was afraid to ask. To this day I am terrible at math. Believing I'm not smart enough was the story I told myself that held me back from getting where I wanted to go.

As a grown woman, I know that not being good at math doesn't mean I am stupid. That was the story I told myself for years. This was so liberating! I wish I had learned it long before my fifties.

Toward the end of my junior year, I had cut class so much that I was in jeopardy of graduating with my class in June of '85. As I sat there in that meeting with my mom and the principal, I felt worthless and believed I would never amount to anything. The principal gave us some choices: go to summer school (God no!), drop out (nope!), or go to continuation school. My mom's idea of continuation school was that people got into fights there and were all bad. I was open to the idea of continuation school, and with the suggestion of my principal, my mom warmed up to the idea too.

We met with the principal of Fairview High, the continuation school in Chico, and enrolled me right away. The super cool thing about continuation school is that you can choose between the morning or afternoon session, and each session is only three hours—sign me up! School for me started at 8 a.m., and I was out at 11! At the time, I worked at Burger King, and all my friends would go there for lunch, so I still got to see them from the cash register when they placed their orders.

I thrived at Fairview! They didn't do lectures and gave me a six-week packet, and if I had questions, I went up to the teacher and asked in private. I went from failing to straight A's. My confidence grew, and when I graduated from Fairview, I received one of two scholarships they offered.

One day in class, my English teacher told me, "Beckie, you are an excellent writer, and you really need to write a book." I looked at her like she just spoke Chinese to me. She was completely serious and believed in me. For the first time in my life, I had a teacher who believed in me! Seriously, no teacher had ever encouraged me to do or be better.

I went to beauty college to get my manicurist license right out of high school. I learned the skill very quickly and was able to build a clientele right away. I got to meet new people who were educated, well-traveled, and wealthy. These women would pay to sit with me for an hour while I did their nails or toes, and I drank from them like a thirsty person who had been stuck out in the desert for months. I listened very carefully to how they spoke, the words they used, and how they lived their lives. Growing up, we didn't have a lot of money, which was okay. Working in a high-end salon, I knew I wanted to create a better life for myself, and I was on my way.

As a little girl, I always knew I wanted to go to beauty college. My dream was to work in Hollywood and be a manicurist for the stars.

My weight was down, I was making money, and I felt great about myself! At 19, this was the BEST I had felt in my skin throughout all my teen years. I was on top of the world!

REFLECTIVE QUESTIONS

1. How is your relationship with food?
2. What encouraging words would you say to your 14-year-old self?
3. What comes to mind when you think about healing the younger version of yourself?

Chapter 4

THE COST OF OBSESSING OVER OUR APPEARANCE

O ur obsession with our appearance comes at a cost. For everything, there is a cost and benefit. Here are a few of the costs:

Poor Self-Esteem: Focusing too much on our appearance can lead to poor self-esteem and negative self-talk. We become hypercritical of ourselves and our bodies, which can spill over into other areas of our lives. It goes back to if my thighs were thinner/toned/perfect, my life would be perfect.

Disordered Eating: Many people who are unhappy with their appearance turn to extreme dieting and other forms of disordered eating to try to control their bodies. This can lead to serious mental and physical health problems.

Missed Opportunities: When we're focused solely on our appearance, we may miss out on opportunities and experiences that could enrich our lives. We may avoid social events or job interviews because we feel self-conscious about our bodies.

What comes to mind are all the photos I chose not to be in when I was heavy and all the pool invites I declined because I didn't want anyone to see me in my swimsuit. Parties I missed because I didn't have anything that fit, or I went out and purchased something just to "fit in," and no one even noticed what I was wearing; they simply enjoyed my company.

There's another consequence that most overlook, and that is it's exhausting to obsess over our bodies! It takes precious energy that could be used elsewhere. If you could take 24 hours off loathing or obsessing over your body, what would be different? Did your shoulders go down? Did you let out a sigh of relief? If you answered yes to either of those questions, you are using precious energy that is wearing you down. Let that $#!+ go.

You might be saying, that's easier said than done, Beckie, and to that, I say, nope, you can let it go. Now, you may be asking, how?

Think about your obsession, or if you feel that's too strong a word, your thoughts directed toward your body that are not positive. What if every time you catch yourself thinking a negative thought about your body, you change it to gratitude? Gratitude heals, and in my opinion, it is a miracle drug.

When you find yourself thinking, *Ugh, my thighs are so fat, covered in cellulite, or ugly,* switch it to *My legs are so strong, and I am grateful to them for carrying me through life.* Or *My arms are so jiggly.* Switch it to *I am so grateful I have arms to hug the people I love so dearly.* Instead of *My butt is so big,* flip it to *I have a cushion for when I sit down.* You get the picture.

Find the gifts in your body. You were not put on this earth to put down your body.

The thoughts are already there; this is reframing them to instill a more positive body image. It takes time to get in the habit of doing it regularly, just as it took time for you to start bashing yourself. You did not come out of the womb hating your thighs, I promise you! Who doesn't love those nice, big, chunky thighs on a baby? I mean, really, who?

Right now, take a moment to write down some things that you say to yourself that are not so nice. Then, reframe them to a more positive saying ... I'll wait.

Here are a few of mine:

I am grateful for strong legs. I am grateful for a sexy round butt. I am grateful for the thick, strong calves that support my frame.

Now that you have a few reframes, wait, did you really do that, or are you sitting there saying I'll do it later? If that's the case, I believe if you do it now, then you know it will be done. I'll wait.

Okay, now that you really have a list of reframes, how can you set some reminders? Here are some ways I set reminders: Post-It notes, messages on my mirror, alarms on my phone, and my phone screensaver.

You may be thinking, *I don't want others to see my notes to myself. I may feel embarrassed, or they may think less of me.* To that, I say, have you been reading the same book here!? BE the change you want to see in the world. Inspire your friends and family to do the same.

Do you have a friend who every time you get together, you both talk about how fat you are or how horrible your body looks? Give them a copy of this book and then ask them to support you in your new way of talking to yourself. They will most likely thank you. If they don't, you may want to question your friendship. It's possible that bashing each other is the only thing you have in common, and once that's removed, the friendship has no legs to stand on and dissolves. In that case, you are better off for it. Find new friends who support you in growing your self-image.

As I get older and I'd like to believe more mature, I see how some friendships expire, and man, it is hard for me to accept that one. I want to hang on! What about all of our history? All the laughs! All of the secrets we share. History smistory, if they aren't part of my new positive self-improvement plan today, they may not be tomorrow either. Love them from afar. If they come around, embrace them. If they don't, send them off with love.

After I learned to love my body, I made a new friend who felt the same about hers, and one day, after knowing her for about four years, I mentioned something about loving my body and how I used to loathe it. She said something so interesting that it has stuck with me since. She said, "I don't know if I would have been friends with you if you complained about your body all the time." Really? That was my response.

It made me wonder how many people, good people, I turned away while loathing my body and focusing on all my perceived flaws. Again, such a waste of time!

When people complain about their bodies and don't do anything about it, it's annoying. Here's what's annoying … it's not that they aren't doing anything about their body; it's the complaining that's annoying. Accept this is your body, period. From there, you can make changes or not. The acceptance part is the first step and, in my opinion, the most important.

Now, you may be thinking, well, when I'm thinner, I can love my body. Or, when I'm in better shape, I can love my body. It's a trap! It's a trap that steals your joy, robs you of creating fun memories, and takes from your life in a way that you can never get back.

Do you think any of the people on the planes that went down on 9-11 thought, *Gosh, I wish I had a thinner body, or I had toned arms?* NO! They were probably thinking about loved ones and the memories they created by being present and involved.

I believe that the sooner you love the skin you are in, the better your life will be and who you attract into it. My friend who said she wouldn't have been my friend if I complained about my body has been one of my closest friends, and I can't imagine my life without her!

The outside of our bodies can and will change. For the most part, the insides do not. Thick or thin, you are still the same awesome person.

Have you ever had a friend complain and never do anything about it? Yup, that's what I am talking about. It is so annoying!

Maybe you are one who suffers in silence. I see you; I used to be that person. I believed that if I never mentioned it to anyone, it would just go away. Ha! It is so funny to type that, as I have never admitted it to anyone. There you go, I shared it with you. I trust you will keep that a secret.

I believed if I didn't say it out loud, I wouldn't have to do anything about it. That sounds so crazy and illogical and yet, that is what I believed. I think I just grew a little bit by sharing that with you.

Sharing how you feel about your body can be healing as long as it's constructive. A constructive share might sound like: "I'm not sure if I can lift that box as my strength has decreased." Non-constructive share: "I am so weak it's pathetic."

Releasing the valve of carrying your thoughts about your body can be freeing. And you never know who you will permit to do the same.

REFLECTIVE QUESTIONS

1. Have you been the annoying friend who always complains about their body and doesn't do anything about it? Or do you have a friend who always complains about it?

2. What opportunities or experiences have you missed out on because of your self-consciousness about your appearance?

3. How have your relationships been affected by your focus on your physical appearance?

Chapter 5

THE DAY I SOLD MY SOUL

When I was 19, I was thin, making great money doing nails, and feeling on top of the world! One night, I went cruising the Esplanade in Chico, California, and I spied a jacked-up silver Toyota with a gorgeous dark-haired man driving and set my sights on him. There was an instant mutual attraction between Tom and me. He was from the Sacramento area and was visiting Chico for the weekend, staying at his parent's cabin up in the hills above Paradise. Right away, I was head over heels for him.

He had a job and a car, which was more than most guys I was meeting! It was love! Tom took me to concerts, nice dinners, and the movies. We had fun together! He was three years older than I was and could legally buy booze. With Tom, I did hold out longer than most to have sex and that made me feel in control and I respected that about myself.

As much as my confidence attracted Tom to me, it was also what he wanted to kill in me. One day, he said, "You look great!" and in my smug feeling good about myself way, I said, "I know." Well, he didn't like that. He didn't like it so much that he withheld compliments as punishment toward me. This created a need for me to get validation from him. I needed to know he thought I was beautiful. He would say it very infrequently, and I lapped it up like a baby bird being fed by its mother every time he gave me the slightest compliment.

This didn't happen overnight; it started out slowly and not obviously. My spirit didn't go down without a fight, although it did go down.

One weekend, after we had been dating for about a year, he took me to a special place and sat me down on this rock on top of a mountain overlooking all of Butte County. It was beautiful, and he told me it was his favorite spot. He set it up so nicely that I believed he was about to propose marriage. Suddenly, I got nervous and wondered how he'd ask and what I would say back. We had talked about marriage, and honestly, I didn't see it coming this day.

It turns out I was wrong, horribly wrong.

Instead, he told me he wanted to propose to me and he really loved me. However, the reason he isn't is because I am too heavy, and if I would lose a little weight, he would then love me enough to spend the rest of his life with me. I sat there in total shock and just stared at him. I was crushed, heartbroken, and embarrassed.

As he drove me home, I quietly cried in the passenger seat next to him and he had no idea. Before arriving at my house, I cleaned up the mascara running down my cheeks and put a smile on my face before saying goodbye to him.

Tom was coming back the following weekend, and I decided I would write him a letter and let him know how hurtful he was and that if he wanted a skinny girl, he would need to find someone else because I was not going to stand for that. I really let him have it in the letter!

I put pen to paper, laid it all out there, and really stood up for myself. After writing, reading, and rereading, I was happy with it. I was standing up for myself proudly!

Upon arrival, I handed him the letter and immediately regretted it.

What had I done? This man was willing to marry me; all I had to do was lose a little weight. I could do that. Thoughts of, *Who else will want me?* came to mind.

To this day, I will never forget his face as he read it. The color left his round cheeks. His smile completely turned into a frown. He was visibly upset, and I caused it. *How could I have been so stupid,* I thought. Right away, I believed I needed to fix this so I didn't lose him. I believed no one else would want me.

When he finished, I immediately told him I was sorry and didn't mean it. I told him if he wanted me to lose weight, I would and how much I loved him. I begged for his forgiveness. That weekend, I did all I could to win him back, and it worked. He won, and in the end, I lost. I lost myself.

Tom and I got married after being together for less than two years. Even though that wedding was almost 36 years ago, I remember it as clear as day. Right as I was about to walk down the aisle, I hyperventilated, and my bridesmaids in front of me slowly backed up, turned around, and looked at me. "Are you okay?" they asked. That was my sign, and I ignored it. I remember looking over and seeing my dad's face, and it went white as a sheet. He had no idea how to help me or what to say. My friends were shocked.

After I composed myself, I took the walk to my fate.

The ceremony was short and sweet, and we had a taco bar followed by a custom three-tiered cake.

I felt so pretty on our wedding day, and Tom never mentioned it. Not before, during, or after.

During the two and a half years we were married, my weight went up and down. Let's be clear here: my highest weight was around 132. He would withhold sex at that weight. He would ask me if I was going to exercise after eating. If he thought I was eating too much at one meal, he would voice it. "Are you going to eat all of that?" he'd ask as I cringed thinking, yes, I am hungry, and now that you asked, my stomach is upset, and I want to please you, so no, no I won't be eating all of that. He won. I lost.

I became so self-conscious while eating that I didn't know if I was hungry or full.

One time, we went to an ice cream shop with my parents at an old favorite place in Chico, and Tom disapproved of my choice as I sat there and ate the whole thing. Did I enjoy it? Not at all! I walked the two miles home in sandals in the middle of a hot summer just to appease him and punish myself.

When he got home, I felt ashamed and embarrassed. He was pleased that I walked it off.

Since Tom worked the night shift, I had dinner by myself during the week. One night, I got some fast food, and although I was good about putting my wrappers in the outside dumpster before he saw them, that night I forgot. He woke me from a sound sleep to angrily ask, "You ate fast food?!" Then he asked, "What about your diet?"

This made me feel shameful as if I needed to justify my actions and choices. "Yes. And it was good" was my only reply.

When I wasn't with him, I thought of food all the time and wondered what I would eat next. My obsession with food was a huge distraction and would interfere with conversations. Tom and I would be talking, and I was thinking about what was in the fridge or if I needed to go to the market to get some candy and eat it in the car on the way home without him knowing.

He would search my car for wrappers, so I learned to drop them off at dumpsters or garbage cans between the store and home.

We bought a house together in Chico, and he voluntarily got laid off from his job so he wouldn't have a 70-minute commute each way. During the day, he would go on bike rides, go to the movies, watch *Geraldo*, and after a 10-hour day, I would come home and cook dinner. He had no plans of finding a job or doing anything to take care of our home. He wouldn't cook, clean the house, or help me in any way. When it came to house chores, he was completely helpless and clueless.

Month after month, the resentment grew, and I could barely look at him without wanting to scream, "What's wrong with you; are you a complete idiot?"

One thing I know for sure about myself is that when I am done with something, I am done!

The day I told him I was leaving, I walked out and never looked back. It was not surprising to him when I told him I no longer respected him; my guess is he lost respect for himself too. The saddest part of that divorce was his mom. She loved me so much, and I adored her! He was her only child, and she had always wanted a daughter. She treated me as if I was her own, and gave me "mad money" for shopping. Our talks were special. She was heartbroken when she got the news and secretly told me she completely understood my decision.

About two years after I left him, I realized I had been in a verbally abusive relationship.

During the marriage, I honestly had no idea it was abuse or withholding. None!

Some may say I was a victim. I believe I chose Tom because, at the time, I didn't believe I could get anyone better, and I don't look back with regret. What the experience did for me was to help me learn what I will tolerate and what I won't. I found great strength in standing up for myself and leaving.

I wish Tom well and remember that we did have a lot of fun together.

REFLECTIVE QUESTIONS

1. Have you ever stayed in a relationship that was unhealthy?
2. Have you ever walked away from a relationship that was unhealthy?
3. Who do you know who is struggling in an unhealthy situation that could use some encouragement?

Chapter 6

WHY WOMEN ALLOW MEN TO DICTATE THEIR HAPPINESS

*A*fter my marriage to Tom ended, I came to a painful realization: he had been verbally abusing me about my body and my weight. This abuse left me deeply scarred, and I believe many women can relate to this experience. This chapter explores why women often allow men to dictate their happiness and how we can reclaim our self-worth and autonomy.

THE SCIENCE BEHIND DEPENDENCY ON EXTERNAL VALIDATION

To understand why women might allow men to dictate their happiness, it's important to delve into the psychological and sociocultural factors at play.

Social Conditioning: From a young age, many women are conditioned to seek approval and validation from others, particularly men. This conditioning can come from various sources, including family dynamics, media portrayals, and societal expectations. Women are often taught that their worth is tied to their appearance and their ability to please others, which can lead to an over-reliance on external validation.

Attachment Theory: Attachment theory, developed by John Bowlby, suggests that early relationships with caregivers shape our expectations and behaviors in adult relationships. Women who experience insecure attachment in childhood may develop patterns of seeking validation and approval from their partners as a way to feel secure and valued.

Self-Esteem and Self-Worth: Low self-esteem and a lack of self-worth can make women more susceptible to allowing others to dictate their happiness. When a woman does not recognize her intrinsic value, she may look to her partner to provide the affirmation she lacks internally. This dependency can lead to a cycle of seeking approval and feeling unworthy without it.

Power Dynamics: In many relationships, power dynamics play a significant role. Men who are controlling or abusive often exert power over their partners by undermining their self-esteem and autonomy. This control can manifest through verbal abuse, manipulation, and other forms of emotional abuse, making it difficult for women to recognize their worth and independence.

My marriage to Tom was a learning chapter in my life. His constant verbal abuse about my body and weight eroded my self-esteem and left me feeling unworthy and unloved. I allowed his words and actions to dictate my happiness because I believed his validation was essential to my self-worth. It wasn't until our marriage ended that I began to see the extent of the damage and the need to reclaim my happiness on my terms, as well as reclaim my body!

By understanding the psychological and sociocultural factors that allow others to dictate our happiness, we can break free from these patterns and reclaim our sense of self-worth and autonomy. Remember, your happiness is your own, and you have the power to create a life that reflects your true value and potential. Embrace your journey of self-discovery and empowerment, and let go of the need for external validation. You are worthy of love and happiness just as you are.

REFLECTIVE QUESTIONS

1. What patterns of seeking validation from others have you identified in your past relationships, and how have they impacted your happiness and self-worth?

2. How can you build your self-worth from within and develop a strong sense of self that is not dependent on external validation?

3. What boundaries can you set in your relationships to protect your emotional well-being and ensure that your happiness is not dictated by others?

Chapter 7

IS IT GETTING HOT IN HERE?

When my divorce was final, I started dating. Keep in mind that I went from living with my parents to living with Tom, so this was the first time I had ever lived alone or with a roommate. My friend Tina, who was also going through a divorce at the time, and I moved into a two-bedroom, two-bath apartment. We set up our place with what we each had to create a cute, homey environment.

At the time, I had several single friends who liked to go out to the bars in downtown Chico.

One night, my friend Sara and I went to the Monte Vista nightclub, and as we walked up the stairs, I looked to my right and gasped. I said to my friend, "That is the most handsome black man I have ever seen in my entire life." It was my mission that night to meet him. He was all alone and easily approachable.

After a drink or two, we made our way to his side of the bar, and I said hello. He smiled with a beautiful set of sparkling white teeth and the most adorable dimples I've ever seen, and it might have been love at first sight. He was friendly, letting us know he had just moved to town, and his birthday was the next day, February 2. His name was Michael, and he was single. Uh, hello!

Michael asked me to dance while a fast song was playing, and as soon as we got onto the dance floor, the music stopped and went into a slow song. As we danced to Marvin Gaye's "Sexual Healing," I thought *Holy smokes, this guy is SO HOT.* I thought my head might explode!

Before that last call for alcohol, Sara and I went to the lady's room. I said to her let's see if we can have a birthday party for Michael the next night. She agreed that would be a great idea and a super slick way to see him again.

The next night, Sara and another friend, Samantha, came over to decorate for Michael's birthday party. Samantha, who was always up for fun, agreed to join us even though she hadn't met Michael. I made chicken enchiladas, baked a cake, and we sang Happy Birthday to him as he blew out his candles. While in his presence, I got weak in my knees and felt like the stupidest things were coming out of my mouth. I guess they didn't bother him because after that night we started dating.

There was one downside. Michael was not willing to commit to a relationship with me. I was not dating anyone else and didn't think he was either, although I wasn't positive and he was a bit secretive. His unwillingness to commit made me feel desperate and clingy. When we were together, I tried to play it cool and act like I wasn't desperate, and I'm not sure if he saw through that.

One thing I did know for sure was that Michael loved my body! He loved every curve and made me feel sexy. For the first time in my life, I felt sexy. All my insecurities I had when I was with Tom about my thighs and big butt had started to dissipate with Michael. Even before we were intimate, he touched my body like it was precious and treasured.

One night, after going out to dinner, Michael and I went back to my apartment, and I walked out of my bathroom into my bedroom to see him lying on my bed face down completely naked. His beautiful black body was in my bedroom lying naked in my bed. The breath completely left my body as I stood there, paralyzed, wondering what action to take. Did he mean to take off all his clothes? Why didn't he get under the covers? What was happening? The only sound I could mutter from my mouth was, "Wow." His reply was, "Is this okay?"

Okay!?! Are you kidding me? As I walked over to my bed, encouraging my body to regain its normal breathing pattern, he looked at me and smiled that phenomenal grin. We made love that night and again the next morning. He was gentle, generous, and loved every single inch of my body. He loved my big butt and hips, and my thighs too. All the areas that Tom made me feel ugly and ashamed about he loved and found sexy.

I believe Michael came into my life to show me that I was beautiful, sexy, and wanted. He was fun and a bit quirky. We dated for several months and then we slowly stopped calling or seeing each other. No hard feelings; it ran its course.

REFLECTIVE QUESTIONS

1. Do you have a regret that still has a hold on you? How can you finally let it go?

2. Who do you need to forgive to find freedom?

3. What can you do for yourself today that is a kind and loving act?

Chapter 8

PRACTICING SELF-COMPASSION

*W*e're often our own harshest critics. Practicing self-compassion can help you break free from negative self-talk and self-judgment. Treat yourself with the same kindness and compassion you would offer a good friend, your partner, child, or pet. Remember that you're worthy of love and acceptance, regardless of your physical appearance.

THE THREE COMPONENTS OF SELF-COMPASSION

According to Dr. Kristin Neff, a leading researcher on self-compassion, there are three core components to this practice:[3]

> **Self-Kindness:** This involves being gentle and understanding with yourself rather than harshly critical. When you make a mistake or experience a setback, practice responding with warmth and empathy instead of self-judgment.

---

[3] Kristin Neff, "What Is Self-Compassion?," Dr. Kristin Neff, accessed September 29, 2024, https://self-compassion.org/what-is-self-compassion/.

Common Humanity: Recognize that suffering and personal failures are part of the human experience. You're not alone in your struggles. This understanding helps you feel more connected to others and less isolated in your pain.

Mindfulness: Mindfulness is the balanced awareness of your thoughts and feelings without suppressing or exaggerating them. It means acknowledging your pain and suffering without becoming overwhelmed by them. This balanced perspective allows you to respond to your own needs with compassion.

For me, practicing self-compassion means I am no longer striving for perfection. A dear friend says, "It's good enough," when she accepts what is instead of forcing perfection. "It's good enough" is a phrase I say in my head daily.

SUGGESTIONS TO PRACTICE SELF-COMPASSION

Acknowledge Your Pain: The first step in practicing self-compassion is recognizing and acknowledging your pain or discomfort. Allow yourself to feel your emotions without judgment. This might involve saying to yourself, "This is really hard right now," or "I'm feeling hurt and overwhelmed."

Speak Kindly to Yourself: Replace harsh, self-critical thoughts with kind and understanding words. Imagine what you would say to a friend or child in a similar situation, and offer yourself those same words of comfort. For example, instead of thinking, "I'm such a failure," try saying, "I'm doing my best, and it's okay to make mistakes; that's how I become a better human."

Practice Self-Soothing: Engage in activities that soothe and comfort you. This could be taking a warm bath, listening to calming music, or spending time in nature. These actions remind you that you deserve care and tenderness, especially during tough times. This was one of the biggest tools I used to end my eating disorder!

Write a Compassionate Letter: When you're struggling with self-criticism, write a letter to yourself from the perspective of a compassionate friend. Address your feelings and offer words of support and encouragement. This exercise can help shift your mindset from self-judgment to self-compassion. "Dear (insert your name), you are a BADASS Overcomer, and I am damn proud of you!"

Mindful Breathing: Practice mindful breathing to ground yourself in the present moment and calm your mind. Focus on your breath as it flows in and out, and use this time to remind yourself of your inherent worth and humanity.

Forgive Yourself: Understand that everyone makes mistakes and experiences setbacks. Forgiving yourself for your imperfections is a crucial aspect of self-compassion. Release the burden of self-blame, and accept yourself as you are.

Seek Support: Surround yourself with supportive and compassionate people who encourage your self-compassion practice. Share your journey with friends, family, or a therapist who can provide guidance and understanding.

By practicing self-compassion, you can transform your relationship with yourself, fostering a sense of inner peace and resilience. Remember, you are worthy of love and acceptance just as you are, and treating yourself with kindness and compassion is a vital step toward a more fulfilling and balanced life.

REFLECTIVE QUESTIONS

1. In what areas of your life do you tend to be the most self-critical, and how can you apply self-compassion in those situations?
2. How do you feel when you practice self-compassion compared to when you engage in self-criticism? What changes do you notice in your emotional well-being?
3. Reflect on a recent experience where you were hard on yourself. How could you have responded with self-compassion instead, and what impact might that have had on your feelings and actions? Rewrite that story in your mind or on paper.

Chapter 9

MY HIGH SCHOOL CRUSH
JUST WALKED INTO MY LIFE

$\mathcal{M}$y high school crush Sam just walked into my work to see me. He came in to see ME! With his blue eyes and charming smile, he looked right at me and said, "Hi, Beckie." I produced words as best as I could, and somehow, we had a conversation. He said he was walking by, saw me through the window, and wanted to say hi.

As we talked, Sam mentioned he was single. "When did that happen?" I asked. "Oh, a while back," he replied. Holy smokes, I was in luck! Could he possibly want to date me? I mean, really, me? *No way*, I thought!

He asked if I wanted to meet him for a drink sometime, and as casually as I could, I said, "Sure, that sounds fun." Ahhhh, I was giddy inside! Oh, wait, he probably just wants someone to go out with because he's bored or no one else is available. That's the story I was telling myself. He couldn't possibly want to date me. Right?

I was kind of seeing someone else at the time who lived out of state, so I wasn't really available. It was safe, and we had fun together.

Sam started showing signs that he was interested in me, and the other guy turned out to be in a committed relationship, so that was a done deal.

We progressed quite quickly from drinks to dating and then to living together. After about a year of dating, we got married.

The best part about Sam is that he loved my body and had no issue with the lumps and bumps. Oh, and he loved to cook and was great at it!

Sam was an emotionally wounded man that I believed I could "fix." Anyone who believes they can "fix" another human being simply by loving them is sadly mistaken. Only they can do it on their own. Then, and only then, if they are ready and willing. Sam was not; that doesn't mean I didn't try.

Sam had one of those childhoods you only read about. His dad was a drug addict and hallucinated that people were living in the attic. He would make the kids go up there to sprinkle flour to see if there were any footprints. He had a lot of trauma that he hadn't let go of, and since he shared it all with me, it made me feel as though he trusted me and, in a sense, made me feel closer to him. He told stories of how his ex-wife was more about her career than she was about him and how he felt neglected. He was smart and funny and oh so good-looking! His piercing blue eyes looked right into my soul, and I felt a never-ending connection between us. His beautiful dark hair and chiseled jawline made him really easy on the eyes.

Sam was a wounded man that needed rescuing, and I was more than willing to save him! It gave me a purpose. It made me feel and believe that I could be the one who would be there by his side to help him see all of his beauty and potential.

There was a huge flaw in that mindset. He didn't see his potential. In time, I discovered that his M.O. was telling his sob story, and women, including me, would buy into it, and they, too, would believe they could rescue him. He was VERY convincing!

We went to Reno to get married in the same little chapel my parents did so many years prior. I purchased an antique off-white dress at a vintage store and felt so pretty and special when I got dressed in our hotel room to go to the chapel.

As we waited for the elevator door to open, the doors were mirrored, and we stood there looking at our reflection. It was a quiet exchange until he said, "Wow, I look great!" He was talking about himself, not me. He never said anything about how I looked. Not a word!

About six months into our marriage, he decided he wanted to go out to the bars without me. At first, I didn't think anything of it and believed he was having fun, and since he always came home to me, I convinced myself it was okay.

One night, he came home much later than the bars closed and had a super pathetic excuse. This is when I started getting suspicious that he might be seeing another woman. He completely denied it and played it off as if I was imagining it. Things got rocky after that.

The suspicion of Sam seeing another woman triggered all my insecurities, and I did what I knew best: I went on a diet. The Diet Center was still in business, and since that was what I knew, I returned. My weight at the time was around 138, and since I was so worried that Sam would leave me, it was easy to lose weight because I could hardly eat anything.

One weekend, I felt I needed to get away and went to visit a friend in Petaluma, which was three hours away. Over that weekend, I reflected on my commitment to the marriage and was unsure what I would find when I got home.

As I walked in the door of our townhouse, it was obvious he had moved out. He left the world's most pathetic note, and needless to say, I was pissed! Also, he took the only lamp in the living room. Who does that!?!

In retaliation, I drove right to Target to buy a lamp, and the unsuspecting cashier got an earful.

It didn't take long for me to find where he moved (he left a newspaper behind with a "room for rent" circled, so maybe he wasn't so smart). I tracked him down and confronted him.

He left me for another woman. He didn't see anything wrong with it. In fact, he justified it by saying I wasn't good to him. I did purchase a car without consulting him, and I believe that was what shifted our relationship.

To say he was angry about my purchasing the car would be an understatement. He yelled so loudly at me my hair flew backward.

I pleaded with him at his doorstep to give me another chance, to give us another chance. He halfheartedly agreed to give our marriage another try.

An opportunity opened for a fresh start. My good friend's sister-in-law wanted to stop doing nails in Petaluma while she stayed home with her kids, and she needed someone to take over her clients. I was 28, and Sam was 31, and we decided we would move to

Petaluma together. Sam applied for a job with a local dairy company delivering milk to markets and was offered it right away. He was one of 75 applicants. He did not immediately accept the job. This was a red flag that I chose not to see.

In December 1995, I packed up and moved to Petaluma. Sam told me to go ahead and move, and he would be there the following month. He needed to give notice and was nervous about it. The next month came, with no notice. Remnants of a previous pattern were showing up again.

One Saturday in February 1996, I was getting ready to drive to Chico to spend the weekend with Sam, and I called him to say I was leaving and when to expect me to arrive. This was before cell phones. His reply was, "Don't bother."

"Um, excuse me?" I said, surprised.

"Don't bother. I don't want to be with you any longer." And he hung up.

He dumped me AGAIN! He never ended the relationship with the other girl. It was me he didn't want, not the other woman! I don't know if I ever knew her name.

He was done. He wanted a divorce. I had no control over the situation and panicked. I was pissed! I was angry and wanted revenge. I wanted him to suffer as he made me suffer. He simply moved on. Eventually, he left her for another woman too.

My marriage was over just like that. Done! He no longer wanted me. All I could think was he didn't want me. No matter how often I told myself I was better off, or others would say, "Forget about him" (by the way, that is horrible advice), all I could think was that he didn't want ME!

It took me about two years to get over him and what he did to me. Not that I hung on to wanting to be with him. What I struggled with was how I felt as a woman. It felt like I was just tossed away like yesterday's leftovers, which are no longer wanted.

My weight was at an all-time low of 118 pounds. My medium-sized frame looked skeletal. My chest was flat, and my face looked sunken in. I did not look healthy, nor did I feel healthy. Strangely, I was at what was considered a "healthy weight," according to the weight charts.

Twenty years later, at a weekend seminar, I had an epiphany and realized his leaving me made me feel worthless. Yes, still 20 years later, I had an unconscious dialog going on in my head that I was completely unaware of, and in that moment, I was able to reframe it.

Sam left me for another woman; that was a fact, and no one could argue that. The meaning I had been giving it all those years was that I was worthless. When we did the exercise that brought about this realization, I sat there sobbing so hard my body shook. I completely let go of the hold he had on me.

The exercise is fact/meaning, and it's so powerful for almost every struggle one may have. The fact is always neutral, it's the part no one can deny, and, in this case, Sam left me. The meaning I was giving it, which is always made up, ALWAYS, was that I was worthless. The new meaning now is that I am a worthy and lovable woman.

The day I let it go, I felt as if a wound I didn't even realize I still had was healed.

When I returned from this seminar and shared the experience with my husband, he was shocked that I had this story going around in my head as he saw me as worthy. Now, I did too.

REFLECTIVE QUESTIONS

1. How do you talk to yourself when you're feeling self-conscious or unhappy with your appearance?
2. What self-compassionate phrases or mantras can you use to counter negative self-talk?
3. How can practicing self-compassion improve your relationship with yourself?

Chapter 10

THE NEED TO RESCUE— UNDERSTANDING THE DESIRE TO SAVE

*I*n this book, I am choosing to share my personal journey with body confidence, including my relationships and the deep-seated beliefs that shaped them. A significant part of my journey involved believing that if I rescued my husband, Sam, from all his pain and abusive childhood, then I would be needed, wanted, and valued. This chapter explores why women like me often need to rescue men and how this desire ties into our sense of worth and identity.

Many women who feel compelled to rescue men do so because of underlying emotional and psychological factors that have been ingrained over time. Here are some common roots of the rescue mentality:

> **Nurturing Instinct:** Women are often socialized as caretakers and nurturers from a young age. This instinct, while beautiful in its essence, can sometimes extend beyond healthy boundaries, leading us to take on the role of a savior in our relationships. I believed I could save Sam!

Seeking Validation: For many women, rescuing someone can be a way to feel needed and validated. By fixing someone else's problems, we may hope to prove our worth and secure our place in their lives. This one is the MOST profound! Focusing on someone else's problems takes us away from our own. BOOM! Then we don't need to face our own problems.

Projection of Pain: Women who have experienced their own traumas or insecurities might project their need for healing onto their partners. By helping someone else heal, they may subconsciously attempt to heal parts of themselves. This may spark an aha for some of you reading this. You may have projected your pain by attempting to save someone without knowing it.

Fear of Abandonment: The fear of being alone or abandoned can drive women to stay in relationships where they feel needed. The belief that their partner cannot survive without them can provide a false sense of security and purpose. I believe this is why I fell so hard when Sam left. The rug had been pulled out from under me, and I couldn't stand on my own.

Codependency: Codependent relationships are characterized by one partner enabling the other's unhealthy behaviors. Codependent women may derive their sense of identity and self-worth from their ability to care for and rescue their partner. I am not sure Sam knew what he was doing. I do know it was a pattern for him, and it is his journey to discover, not mine.

My relationship with Sam was a manifestation of many of these factors. Sam had endured a painful and abusive childhood, and I felt an overwhelming need to rescue him from his past. I believed that if I could heal his wounds, I would be indispensable to him. This belief fed into my insecurities and desire for validation.

In trying to rescue Sam, I often neglected my needs and well-being. I became so consumed with fixing his problems that I lost sight of my own value independent of his struggles. It was only later, long after he left me, that I realized this dynamic was unsustainable and unhealthy for both of us.

I also chose Sam over my friendships because I believed if I could be with him all the time, I would have more influence on him. Yikes, that was hard to type. It's hard to recognize the truth.

WHY DO WOMEN FEEL THE NEED TO RESCUE?

Conditioned Roles: Society often conditions women to believe their worth is tied to their ability to care for others. This conditioning can lead to a pattern of seeking out partners who need rescuing, reinforcing the belief that their value lies in their ability to save.

Unresolved Personal Issues: Women with unresolved personal issues, such as low self-esteem or past traumas, might seek out relationships where they can focus on someone else's problems instead of their own. This diversion can temporarily distract from their inner pain. This is truly from a space of subconscious and not conscious. Or at least, it was for me.

Romanticized Notions: Popular culture and media often romanticize the idea of the "wounded" partner who is healed by the love and care of their significant other. This narrative can create unrealistic expectations and desires to be the one who brings about transformation.

Emotional Investment: Women who have invested a lot emotionally into a relationship may feel a sense of duty to rescue their partner. This investment can create a cycle where they feel responsible for their partner's well-being.

Sidenote: I do know that some men rescue women too, and it's probably for all of the above reasons as well as others.

BREAKING THE CYCLE

Recognizing the pattern of needing to rescue is the first step toward breaking the cycle. Here are some strategies to help:

Self-Reflection: Take time to reflect on your motivations and the roots of your rescue mentality. Understanding the underlying reasons can help you address them.

Set Boundaries: Establish healthy boundaries in your relationships. Recognize that while it's okay to support your partner, it's not your responsibility to fix their problems. That last one might hit hard for some.

Seek Support: Therapy or counseling can provide a safe space to explore these dynamics and develop healthier relationship patterns.

Focus on Self-Worth: Work on building your self-esteem and recognizing your worth independent of your ability to rescue others. Engage in activities that bring you joy and fulfillment.

Encourage Self-Reliance: Encourage your partner to seek their own path to healing. Support them, but also empower them to take responsibility for their growth and well-being.

My message to you if you recognize you are in a relationship that is unhealthy and you are rescuing: How you got here was from a place of good intentions, wanting to do the right thing, and being genuinely sincere. Now that you are aware of your desire to save or rescue, I congratulate you. Being aware of it allows you to make some choices from a place of taking responsibility and not being a victim.

You may be unable to leave the relationship due to the situation or money. What you can do now is take the steps to start owning your worth and owning your choices without shame and guilt because that will only keep you stuck.

By understanding why you need to rescue others and addressing the underlying issues, you can cultivate healthier, more balanced relationships. Remember, you are worthy of love and acceptance for who you are, not just for what you can do for others. Embrace your journey to healing and self-discovery, and allow your relationships to be a source of mutual support and growth. This does not happen overnight, and the other party in the relationship may not be on board. Take care of yourself, and the rest will follow.

REFLECTIVE QUESTIONS

1. What past experiences or beliefs have contributed to your desire to rescue others in your relationships?

2. How has the need to rescue affected your own well-being and sense of self-worth?

3. What steps can you take to establish healthier boundaries and focus on your growth and fulfillment?

Chapter 11

THE MASSACRE

n the two years following Sam leaving me, I dated A LOT!

At the time, I didn't realize what I was doing, and I now look back on it with sadness and regret.

I broke a lot of hearts in an attempt to heal my own. For the record, it didn't work, and I do not suggest anyone take this approach.

I would unknowingly seek out men who were kind of desperate, and I knew I could manipulate. They would follow me around like a puppy dog, and I would get my sick and unhealthy fill from it. Well, that was until they started to bug me. That's what I called "The Bug." Once the bug set in, they were toast. Oh, I would let them down nicely with the whole "It's me, not you" thing and then top it off with "Let's be friends."

The bug would set in with things like the way they chewed their food, dressed, or answered the phone … any little annoyance and I gave them the axe!

Although I didn't know it at the time, I was looking for something I wouldn't discover until years later—peace. Peace within myself and who I am. Realize and own my worth. And forgive Sam for being a wounded man who can only heal himself.

Believing that I could rescue a wounded man wasn't selfish or wholesome; it was derived from insecurity and the need to be needed. In my mind, he needed me, and I guess I needed him too.

In all of my dating during this time in my life, there was a shift. The shift came in the form of starting to see my worth, and although I hadn't fully realized it yet, I started setting the bar higher and higher for myself and the men I chose to date.

I still worked at the nail salon in Petaluma, and since it was a small place, everyone knew my dating life. That could also be because I openly shared.

As this shift in me occurred, I dated less and spent more time alone. I was raising my bar both for myself and the men I dated. I was shifting into believing more in myself and my worth.

I enrolled in business college and decided I wanted more for myself. I was worth more!

A lady who was a client of the nail salon where I worked was interested in my dating life. She told me I needed to lower my standards, and that's why I wasn't finding Mr. Right. Um, I don't think that's the direction I want to go with this, but thank you.

REFLECTIVE QUESTIONS

1. Who do you allow to influence you, if anyone?
2. How do you give yourself approval?
3. When was the last time you celebrated a healthy choice you made?

Chapter 12

MY THIGHS WERE STILL IN THE WAY

So how do you shift your focus away from your appearance, or at least the parts you don't like, and onto other aspects of your life? Here are a few steps you can take:

Sidenote: Taking an interest in your appearance is a sign of self-love and acceptance. Please know that I am not suggesting you let yourself go or stop caring about how you look. NOT AT ALL! There's a huge difference between wanting to look nice simply because it feels good to look good versus needing to look good to be loved, have value, or be recognized for your gifts.

CHALLENGE YOUR BELIEFS

Start by questioning the beliefs you have about your appearance and how it relates to your worth as a person. Are these beliefs really true? Are they helping you live your best life?

Did your friend have small thighs when you were growing up, and yours were more like tree trunks, so you compared yourself to her? Just like I did? When I was a pre-teen, my best friend had phenomenal genes with great legs that were naturally toned and completely free of cellulite ... I wanted her legs. Through this comparison, I thought less of my legs and did so for YEARS! Even though my legs are strong and carry me through life, I used to look at them with disgust.

My friend would stand in front of the mirror and pull back the skin on the back of her thighs to see how they would look if they were thinner. "Um, excuse me, they look phenomenal as they are now," is what I was screaming inside my head.

At 33 years old, I decided to have liposuction on my thighs, and to this day, I believe it was a beneficial decision. My body was so out of proportion, with large thighs and a small waist, that finding clothes that fit properly without tailoring was a constant challenge. Ironically, who could have predicted that a trend celebrating small waists and larger butts and thighs would emerge? I certainly didn't see that coming!

I like big butts, and I cannot lie!

Question your beliefs about your body. Are you comparing yours to someone else's? Even with plastic surgery, my thighs would have never looked like my best friend's thighs because we have different genes, period. Having that awareness now as a grown woman seems so obvious to me, and at the same time, it feels so familiar to compare.

Start to get curious about your beliefs around your body, and notice if you compare yourself to others.

In my mid-twenties, I had a friend who grew up as a ballerina, and her legs were toned, defined, and absolutely gorgeous! She carried weight around her middle, and her body was the complete opposite of mine.

She bought a matching red skirt and jacket that she would wear when we went out to the clubs. It was sexy, cute, and stunning. It had ruffles on the neckline and bottom of the skirt. I dreamed of wearing it and looking as good as she did in it.

One day, I got my wish (well, kind of), when she decided it was time for the red skirt and jacket to get donated. To me, it had a lot of life left in it, and I wanted it in my life. Since our bodies were completely the opposite of each other, I made my way to my seamstress.

I donned the suit in my seamstress's office, and it looked a bit like a little girl trying on her mom's clothes. The fit was so wrong.

The seamstress dutifully pinned it in areas where it would need to be taken in or adjusted, and there were a lot of them. Soon, we both realized no matter how many pins she used, this outfit was not going to fit my body, PERIOD!

It was like putting a square peg in a round hole.

Our bodies are unique by design, not by flaws. Let's learn to celebrate that!

Here's a tool that I like to use, and it might be mentioned more than once in this book because, hey, we can all use a reminder. When I catch myself comparing myself to someone, I stop and say quietly, "Comparing." I say this without judgment or shame. It's simply a notice. Then, in that moment, I have a choice to keep comparing OR turn the love to myself and offer up what I am grateful for in my body. When I choose the latter, I walk away feeling so much better about myself.

This also works with judging others.

FOCUS ON YOUR STRENGTHS

Instead of obsessing over your flaws, focus on your strengths. What are you good at? What do you enjoy doing? What makes YOU unique?

A few years ago, there was a movement to "strengthen your weaknesses." I remember reading that and thinking, *Oh boy, I've got a long way to go …*

My guess is the theory behind strengthening your weaknesses is to grow as a human, and I support that 100%! To me, focusing on my weaknesses felt like walking up an escalator that was going down—frustrating, defeating, and not uplifting.

When I shift to focus on my strengths, it feels like running up an upward-moving escalator—exhilarating, exciting, and forward-moving. I love my strengths! They are what makes me, me, the unique me that I am … and the same is true for you.

As much as focusing on your strengths may seem like a mundane or unnecessary step, it's the foundation to loving your body, your life, and your whole person. It starts here (imagine a map at an amusement park that says, "You are here"). Now, highlight all your strengths. Note: this is best done on paper, either handwritten or typed. You can even start a note on your smartphone. This could be a running list where every time you notice a strength, you add to it.

Transitioning your focus from your flaws to your strengths starts the process of loving and accepting the person you see looking back at you in the mirror.

Some of mine are my creativity, humor, interesting perspective, and curiosity in others. Now, start your unique list. Strengths are traits and habits, which can be physical as well.

PRACTICE SELF-CARE

Self-care is about more than just physical appearance. It's about taking care of your mental and emotional health too. Make time for activities that nourish your soul, like meditation, yoga, or spending time in nature (one of my personal favorites).

Self-care is also about consumption. What are you consuming in the way of music, podcasts, TV shows and movies, and social media … what are you consuming with your eyes and ears? Does it lift you up or leave you feeling less than?

My hiking buddies love *True Crime* podcasts. While hiking, they listen to ones about people who go missing while hiking. I do not get this at all! We recently did a road trip, and I listened to a few episodes with them. I did not like how I felt as I heard the stories. The people and what they went through felt like it got inside my body, and I was carrying their trauma with me.

This did not fill me up in a positive way.

Even though it didn't make me feel or think less about my body, it didn't lift me in a way that felt good and positive.

No judgment to my friends or anyone who enjoys *True Crime* podcasts; I know it's not for me. This is self-care.

Choosing what I consume on TV and social media and with whom I spend my time is an active act of self-care, as is speaking up and saying, "I don't want to watch or listen to that" from a place of it's simply not for me, and I am okay with that.

Sure, self-care is also hygiene, eating well, and moving your body.

Self-care and body confidence extend far beyond the basics of hygiene and nutrition; they delve into the profound relationship we have with ourselves. It's about embracing the idea that your body is not just a vessel to be sculpted and perfected but a living, breathing testament to your life's journey. Each scar, stretch mark, and curve tells a story of resilience, growth, and survival.

Recognizing this can be a transformative "aha" moment. Imagine standing in front of a mirror with a compassionate gaze that acknowledges every part of you as a unique expression of your life's experiences and inner strength instead of a critical eye searching for flaws.

Body confidence is also about understanding that true beauty radiates from within. It's cultivated through self-love and acceptance, which flourish when you start to appreciate your body's abilities rather than its appearance. Consider the marvel of your body's functionality: how your legs carry you through life's adventures, how your hands can create and comfort, and how your heart beats tirelessly to sustain you. When you shift your focus from how your body looks to what it can do, you unlock a profound respect and admiration for yourself. This shift in perspective is the cornerstone of genuine body confidence, empowering you to live more freely and fully in your skin.

Additionally, self-care and body confidence are deeply intertwined with the practice of self-compassion and mindful presence. It's about giving yourself permission to feel good about your body without needing external validation. Imagine releasing the weight of societal expectations and the constant comparison to others. Instead, immerse yourself in moments of mindfulness where you truly connect with your body. This could be through gentle stretches that make you aware of your body's strength and flexibility or through quiet moments of gratitude where you thank your body for all it does each day.

Moreover, embracing creativity and self-expression can be a profound way to celebrate your body. Whether through dance, fashion, art, or any other form of expression, engaging in activities that make you feel alive and joyful can reinforce a positive connection with your body. When you honor your body as a source of creativity and joy, you pave the way for a deeper, more loving relationship with yourself.

Ultimately, self-care and body confidence are about cultivating an inner dialogue that is supportive and loving. It's about recognizing that you are more than your physical appearance and that your worth is inherent, not determined by how you look. By nurturing an honoring approach to self-care that includes emotional, mental, and spiritual well-being, you can build a foundation of body confidence that empowers you to navigate the world with authenticity and grace.

REFLECTIVE QUESTIONS

1. What beliefs do you need to challenge to shift your focus away from physical appearance?
2. What are some of your strengths, and how can you focus on them more?
3. What self-care practices can you incorporate into your daily life that don't focus on physical appearance?

Chapter 13

MEETING MR. RIGHT

"He's rustic-looking." That's how Jens was described to me before our blind date in May 2000. After a run of some pretty awful blind dates, rustic-looking didn't sound so bad. Hours before our date, I considered canceling because I wasn't sure if I could go through one more bad date. I chose to go.

On our first date, I knew he was different. He was kind, gentle, and really listened to me. We dated for two-plus years before we got married in a quiet ceremony in my hometown of Chico. My dad, who was to pass away only six weeks later from kidney cancer, was able to walk me down the aisle. He happily gave me away to Jens and knew I was in good hands. As I stood by Jens' side about to say our "I do's," he looked at me and whispered, "You look so beautiful." The third time really is a charm!

Early in our courtship, I knew that I loved Jens; he took a bit longer. At 10 months, I had already used the "L" word, and he said he didn't know if he loved me or could ever love me.

That was when I knew my value and worth. I broke up with him because I knew I was better than that and would always wonder if he loved me. I wasn't willing to take that risk.

We were apart for two and half months—it took that long for him to miss me and realize that he too loved me. We got back together, and I have never doubted his love for me, nor has he given me any reason to doubt.

During our breakup, I gave Love@AOL a go. I connected with a guy, and we met at a restaurant in Petaluma, where we had a nice time. He did not knock my socks off. The funny thing is that during our meal, I excused myself from the table to use the restroom, and on my way there, I saw the man who introduced me to Jens at a table. As I got closer, he was avoiding me like the plague.

It was strange until I got beside his booth and saw him dining with Jens. Right as I walked by, Jens looked in the opposite direction. What the heck?

I went into the bathroom and phoned a friend. We laughed, and when I returned to my table, Jens again had no idea I was there until the next day when a friend of his told him.

Three days later, I had a second date with a Love@AOL guy. He took me to the beach where we attempted to have a picnic and the wind had other plans. The wine was sandy, the conversation was awkward, and all I could think about was I just wanted to be with Jens.

That night, I called him to let him know I had gotten hired for a new job. When I met Jens, I had just started business college and graduated during our breakup. Letting him know I got hired seemed a good reason to phone him.

During our call, we ventured into our breakup, and I asked him why he hadn't called me. He had a reason that didn't please me, and the conversation ended on a poor note.

Fifteen minutes later, there was a knock on my door. It was Jens. He didn't like how our call ended and wanted to make it right. He went on to say that he had missed me every single day of our breakup. I asked him, "What do you think that means?" His reply was, "That I love you." FINALLY!!!

I moved in with Jens right before the holidays in November 2001. We had his mom, sister, and brother-in-law over for a holiday dinner. It was a disaster! The roast was overcooked, the mashed potatoes were tough, and the persimmon pudding wasn't set. When I flipped it over, the liquid went all over the counter. Somehow, they don't remember that dinner the same way I do, and for that, I am grateful.

From day one with Jens, I could truly be myself and felt like I was home. He provided me with safety, security, and commitment. It was like I could fall, and I knew he would catch me.

Since I was 35 and Jens was 47, we tried and successfully got pregnant right away. On July 17, 2003, we had our son, Henry, the pride and joy of my life. This was meant to be the best time of my life, right?

After having my son, I had postpartum depression and did not know it. I remember when he was six weeks old, I was sitting on the toilet feeling so incredibly sad and thought to myself, *How in the world could you possibly be sad?* I had a healthy baby and was able to stay home and take care of him, and my husband was loving and supportive. The sadness grew and grew.

With each day, my binging grew and grew. At no time did I think I was depressed. Honestly, it never crossed my mind. I just thought I was going crazy! This went on for a couple of years.

My binging was around 3:00 in the afternoon. It would start with a snack. "I'm hungry; it's normal to have an afternoon snack," I would justify. The problem was that it was more than a snack. After that "snack," I would eat something else, then more, and more, and more. I would get into a state where I just couldn't stop eating. It felt like I was possessed and had no control over my body and choices. I ate WAY beyond satisfied and into sick to my stomach full. Then, as if someone waved a magic wand over my head, I came to. I woke up and felt sick, guilty, and full of shame.

I would go on to repeat this cycle on a daily basis for the next few years—binge, guilt and shame, binge. Every day, I said to myself, "Not today!" then 3:00 would hit, and BAM, this little voice said, "Snack time!"

My husband and my friends had no idea this was my cycle.

My highest weight when I was pregnant was 196. Through dieting, I got back down to around 140. After pregnancy, my body no longer tolerated "the pill," so I chose an IUD. My OB/GYN assured me weight gain was not a side effect. During the five years it was in, I gained 10 pounds each year. Was it the IUD, OR was it my binging? My best guess is it was both …

REFLECTIVE QUESTIONS

1. When did you stand up for yourself even though you were scared?
2. Have you ever said yes when you wanted to say no?
3. How can you celebrate your self-honoring choices today?

Chapter 14

FINDING JOY BEYOND
YOUR APPEARANCE

*Y*our appearance is just one small part of who you are. You have so much to offer the world beyond your physical appearance. Focus on finding joy in the things that truly matter to you, like spending time with loved ones, pursuing your passions, and positively impacting the world.

It's easy to become consumed by societal standards of beauty and the pressure to look a certain way. However, your true value lies not in how you look but in who you are and what you bring to the world. Embracing your whole self means recognizing that you are a complex, multifaceted individual with a unique combination of talents, passions, and experiences.

FINDING JOY IN RELATIONSHIPS

One of the most profound sources of joy comes from the connections we share with others. Whether it's family, friends, or romantic partners, these relationships enrich our lives in ways that far surpass any physical attribute.

Post pandemic we have a loneliness epidemic, and connection is more important than ever! Maybe you are not lonely; there are people around you who would love to connect with you.

Here are some ways to deepen your relationships and find joy in them:

Quality Time: Spend meaningful time with your loved ones. Engage in activities that you all enjoy, have heartfelt conversations, and be present in the moment. These shared experiences strengthen your bonds and create lasting memories.

Express Gratitude: Regularly express your appreciation for the people in your life. A simple thank you, a heartfelt note, or a kind gesture can go a long way in making others feel valued and loved.

Active Listening: Practice active listening when others are speaking. Show genuine interest in their thoughts and feelings, and respond with empathy and understanding. This fosters deeper connections and also demonstrates that you value them beyond appearances. Put down your phone.

PURSUING YOUR PASSIONS

Engaging in activities that ignite your passion is another powerful way to find joy beyond your appearance. Pursuing your interests and hobbies can bring immense satisfaction and a sense of purpose. Here are some tips for reconnecting with your passions:

Explore New Interests: Be willing to try new things. Whether it's picking up a musical instrument, learning a new language, or exploring a new sport, expanding your horizons can lead to unexpected joys and discoveries.

Dedicate Time: Carve out time in your schedule to engage in activities that bring you joy. Treat these moments as essential parts of your routine, just as important as any other commitment.

Join Communities: Find groups or communities that share your interests. Connecting with like-minded individuals can provide a sense of belonging and mutual support, enhancing your enjoyment and commitment to your passions.

MAKING A POSITIVE IMPACT

Contributing to the well-being of others and the world at large can be incredibly fulfilling. When you focus on making a positive impact, you shift your attention from superficial concerns to meaningful actions. Here are some ways to make a difference:

Volunteer: Offer your time and skills to causes that resonate with you. Whether it's helping at a local shelter, mentoring youth, or participating in environmental cleanups, volunteering can create a sense of purpose and connection.

Advocate for Change: Use your voice and influence to advocate for social, environmental, or political causes that matter to you. Being an agent of change can be empowering and deeply satisfying.

Acts of Kindness: Simple acts of kindness, like helping a neighbor, donating to a charity, or offering a listening ear, can make a significant difference in someone's life. These actions not only uplift others but also enhance your sense of fulfillment.

CULTIVATING A BALANCED LIFE

Finding joy beyond your appearance requires a holistic approach to life. It's about balancing various aspects of your existence—relationships, passions, work, and self-care—in a way that aligns with your values and satisfies you. Here are some strategies to cultivate a balanced life:

Set Priorities: Identify what truly matters to you and prioritize those areas. This may involve setting boundaries, saying no to unnecessary commitments, and focusing on activities that bring you joy and fulfillment.

Practice Mindfulness: Mindfulness helps you stay present and fully engage with whatever you're doing. It allows you to appreciate the moment and find joy in the here and now rather than constantly striving for future perfection.

Self-Reflection: Regularly reflect on your life and assess how well your actions align with your values and goals. Make adjustments as needed to ensure you're living in a way that feels authentic and rewarding.

By focusing on relationships, passions, and positive contributions, you can find joy and fulfillment that transcends physical appearance. Embrace your whole self, celebrate your unique qualities, and live a life rich with purpose and connection. Remember, the true essence of who you are is far more valuable than any external attribute.

REFLECTIVE QUESTIONS

1. What activities or experiences bring you the most joy and fulfillment, and how can you incorporate more of them into your daily life?

2. Think about the people in your life who lift you up and make you feel valued. How can you nurture these relationships and express your appreciation for them?

3. Reflect on a recent moment when you positively impacted someone else's life. How did it make you feel, and how can you create more opportunities to contribute to the wellbeing of others?

Chapter 15

IS THIS NORMAL?

As I sat on the toilet, I thought to myself, what is wrong with me? I have a healthy six-week-old baby. My husband is great, and he loves me. At the time, I didn't need to go back to work, and my days were filled with feedings, naps, diaper changes, and an enormous amount of love for this little baby that I had given birth to.

My husband and I have always sat down to have dinner together, and every night, we would talk about our day. At the time, my day's recall usually started with, "So, today on *Oprah* ..." and he would politely listen and engage in conversation about said topic. Jens would share about his day of farming. If it was an "uneventful" day, that was a good day. No equipment failure or catastrophe made for a smooth and productive day.

One day, in particular, stands out in my memory as it was the day my awareness of my mental state hit me square on the forehead.

When I was watching, you guessed it, *Oprah*, she did a show about actors who were battling depression and anxiety. As I watched and listened to what they were feeling about these conditions, I could totally relate! Sadness. Lack of joy. Heart racing for no reason. Depression. Did I have depression? As I listened to each new story more and more, I identified with each person and realized this is how I have felt ALL my life and thought it was normal.

I honestly believed everyone had irrational thoughts. Everyone wakes up in the middle of the night and worries about a conversation they had four months ago as if it were occurring right now, right?

Hearing this made me both excited and scared. If I'm depressed, then what? Do I see a shrink? Do I need to be on meds? Will my son get this? Is there help for me?

That night at the dinner table, I decided to tell Jens my new findings and share how I'd been feeling.

One of the biggest AHAs I had while watching *Oprah* was that not only was I depressed, I had also learned to be really good at hiding it. So when I told Jens, he was surprised. He was unaware of the deep, dark feelings I was having.

A couple of years prior to this conversation, a woman, Andrea Yates, who was severely depressed, drowned all five of her children in the bathtub on June 20, 2001. I believe *Oprah* did a show on it. That left a mark on both my husband and me, and he asked if I considered hurting our child. This woman said the voices in her head kept telling her to do this. She was diagnosed with severe postpartum depression, postpartum psychosis, and schizophrenia. She was sentenced to life in prison, which was later overturned because of a false testimony by an expert witness.

In the retrial, they found her not guilty by reason of insanity. She will be staying in a high-security mental hospital for the rest of her life.

The newly discovered mental health awareness was not taken lightly by me or my husband. Although I knew I could never hurt or harm my son, I thought there once was a time that Andrea Yates thought the same thing too.

The best way I can describe how I felt is that I could just lie down on the floor at the grocery store. Although I'm not an extreme germophobe, in my right mind, I would NEVER allow myself to lay on the floor anywhere in public, let alone the grocery store. In my intense sadness, I felt like the ground was sucking me in, and I had concrete for feet. Every step I took felt like a monumental feat.

When Jens was home, I did my absolute best to hide it, and when I was around others, I learned to put a smile on my face and just "suck it up."

Jens was so supportive of my getting the help I needed that it allowed me to fall, and when I say fall, I mean fully into the depths of depression. For the first time in my life, I truly felt safe, loved, and free to fall. Once I let out how I was feeling, I became more and more aware of how long I had been feeling this way. Without a doubt, I had postpartum depression.

A trip to a psychiatrist would confirm this and give me hope.

Fortunately, we have great medical coverage, and Kaiser takes mental health seriously. It took a few weeks, though, before I could get in to see a therapist. I was nervous. Even though I have seen therapists over the years, this time was different. I had a child who needed me and a husband who wanted me at my best to take care of both of them.

As I sat there in that office with the therapist, she asked a lot of questions, which I answered honestly and to the best of my ability.

She was the person who was assessing me to see where I would go next. She looked at me and said, "Beckie, you have anxiety and a touch of OCD."

"Um, anxiety?" I asked. I thought it was depression. Boy, did I learn a whole lot about anxiety AND depression after that appointment. And let's not gloss over the OCD; I'll get to that later.

If you do not have anxiety, then you are really lucky!

What I came to learn is anxiety is this crazy reaction to nothing. Yup, nothing. That's my best description of it. There would be times when I would be sitting and relaxing with no danger or stress, and suddenly, my heart would race, my stomach would knot, and I would enter panic mode as if I were being chased by a pack of wild animals. That was only one symptom of anxiety; there were and are so many more!

It turns out that "normal" people don't lie in bed in the middle of the night and worry (more like panic) about a conversation they had months ago. Worry, gosh, don't even get me started on the constant worry! Strange thoughts would enter my mind as I was driving, like what if I drove off the side of the road and hit that pedestrian? Irrational thoughts were constantly going through my mind, and it was EXHAUSTING! Enter depression.

Being all hyped up from anxiety takes a lot out of you because you can be in this state for days or even weeks. When you come down from anxiety, you enter depression. In my opinion, it's as if your body says, "I really need a break, so I'm going to slow you the heck down."

The grocery store floor feeling was depression that was brought on by anxiety. Whew, I had some answers … next, let's try some meds. Yes, I chose to start with meds.

At first, I was super reluctant to go on meds because of the rumors. Will I go numb and never feel emotions? Will I be a zombie? Will they help?

The first meds prescribed made me feel like I just did 14 lines of cocaine, and I was supposed to take it morning and night. Just one time, and I said, "No, thank you!" Next …

The next one worked! By worked, I mean about three or four weeks after starting Zoloft, the clouds suddenly lifted, and I felt what I described as "normal." I had focus and great attention—this was so cool! I could actually have a conversation with someone and pay attention to what they were saying. Little things no longer bugged me. I didn't wake up in the middle of the night worrying about previous conversations. For literally the first time in my entire life, I felt normal. A huge cause for celebration!

Having an awareness that I had anxiety all my life made so much sense to me. The paranoia. Year after school year I worried that my prior teacher told my current teacher about me. I'm not sure what I believed they told them, I just knew it was bad, that I was bad.

Dwelling on small stuff was no longer my focus, and this gave me more energy. I loved being on Zoloft … until …

With Zoloft and all anti-anxiety medications, there are side effects. The funny thing about these drugs is they affect everyone differently, and you don't know how you will be affected until you use them for a while.

There were two major side effects for me. One was dry mouth. I was thirsty all the time! My dentist told me that dry mouth can increase plaque, tooth decay, and gum disease. These were livable in my mind because my anxiety was completely under control.

The second side effect was not so great. I had difficulty reaching orgasm. By difficult, I mean it was a no-go. No matter how close I would come, nope, it would not happen. If I couldn't reach orgasm, it kind of made me depressed ... are you with me on this? It was not going to work.

My doctor suggested we try a different medication, and I was mildly willing. With the memory of the one that made me feel like I had snorted a bunch of cocaine, I was nervous, to say the least.

The third medication made me feel more depressed.

You've heard people say, "Oh, I felt better, so I stopped taking my meds ..." That was sort of me. I decided I no longer needed to take anti-anxiety medication and could just figure it out. I did taper off responsibly.

My husband, son, and I went to Fort Bragg for a few days to ride the Skunk Train. We were sitting in the train station waiting for our train to arrive so we could board and go for a beautiful trip through the redwoods. As I sat there, with more than enough time until we were to board, I had the biggest anxiety attack I had ever had. For no reason, absolutely no reason at all! As I sat there with my heart racing as if hungry wolves were going to eat my family and me, I felt defeated, frustrated, and broken.

When we returned from our trip, I knew I didn't want to go back on the meds. They had left my body, and things were much better in the bedroom, success!

One night, while I lay in bed, I prayed so hard for God to bring me a miracle to rid me of this curse. Something that would give me relief so I wouldn't have to go back on the meds and could be normal again. Please, God, please, I said in desperation.

The next morning, I got up, and as I sat on the couch with my coffee, I turned on the TV. Lo and behold, there was an infomercial on how to overcome anxiety and depression. God came through! Since my son was sitting next to me, I didn't want him to see or hear it, so I recorded it and watched it later by myself.

The infomercial was for a place called The Midwest Center, founded by Lucinda Bassett. There was a number you could call to talk to an agent, and I dialed the phone with anticipation, hoping this was my answer. A man answered, asked me some questions about what was going on, and told me he believed this program would help me. Although somewhat skeptical, I gave him my credit card. He told me I would get one 60-minute coaching session as a gift.

About a week later, my box of hope arrived. The program came with a book that corresponded with 15 weekly CDs. From the first meditation CD, I knew this was special. Something was happening; I was changing.

The free coaching session I got was so helpful I decided to pay to have a coach weekly for 15 weeks. This proved to be an excellent investment! Getting to talk openly about my anxiety was so freeing. My coach had overcome anxiety through the program and helped me to do the same.

In just 15 weeks, I can honestly say I left my anxiety behind. It was a miracle. No meds! No more worrying! No crazy thoughts! Well, I had crazy thoughts, and the program taught me to see them with humor, which took away all the power they had held over me.

That was in 2012, and I can say I no longer have anxiety. However, a very difficult life event did bring it on again in 2018, which you'll read about later.

Note: Since I did The Midwest Center program, Lucinda Bassett sold the company. The new name is Stress Center, and it still has the 15-week program I mentioned. The name of it is "Attacking Anxiety and Depression Drug-Free," and it will run you about $129. If you can swing it, get the coaching too.

REFLECTIVE QUESTIONS

1. Do you know someone who has anxiety or depression that you can give more grace to today?
2. How can you incorporate more fun into your life?
3. What can you do today to spread more joy into your life?

Chapter 16

I HAVE A WHAT?

*S*ince that moment in the pantry with Ritz crackers and cheese at 13, I binged off and on. More on than off. During this "on" time, I was binging daily and had been for a few years.

It was mid-December, and my husband was home from work that day. My normal binge time came, and I completely panicked! He was in his favorite recliner, right next to the kitchen where my afternoon fix was. When I say I panicked, I mean like a crack addict jonesing for the "goods." That panic sent me into an anxiety attack, and from there, I got scared. "What the heck is wrong with me!?!"

In that moment, I knew I HAD to get help! Where? Who could I turn to that wouldn't judge or make me feel even more shame than I already felt? WHO?!

During a routine appointment with my doctor, she asked about my eating. At the time, I was around 180, and at 5' 1.5", that is considered obese. As I reluctantly told her about my afternoon "snack" that turned into out-of-control eating beyond the comfortable state (I may have held back on how extreme it was), she looked at me and said, "It sounds like you have an eating disorder."

My jaw hit the floor. But I don't stick my finger down my throat! But I'm not anorexic! But … but … but … what?! No, I believed I was just lazy with no self-control or willpower. It was all my fault that I couldn't control myself.

My doctor said, "The way you eat is disordered, and it has now been recognized as an official eating disorder called binge eating disorder, or BED." This was around 2009, I believe.

Eating disorder means disordered eating … who knew?

My doctor went on to say there was an ongoing eating disorder class that I could get into right away.

As I drove home that day, processing this information and settling into the fact that I had an eating disorder, I wanted to keep it quiet AND shout it out loud at the same time. I had so many questions and, at the same time, felt I also got so many answers as so much made sense now.

That night, I decided to tell my husband, and I was scared to death! As I sat there shaking and spilling all my food secrets, he listened lovingly and quietly. He had no idea that I was binging during the day. How could he since I did it all in hiding? I was a classic closet eater. In public, it looked like I hardly ate anything, and in private, I could take out enough food for a growing teen boy and then some.

Sharing with my husband relieved a bit of guilt and shame. Letting my secret out helped a little bit. It was like the valve that I had screwed on so tightly was slightly released. It felt as though I could breathe a little easier. It felt a lot like hope.

The next month, I went to my first eating disorder class. Before I left the house, I joked to my husband that I was going to the "fatty" class. This was my way of inserting humor to make it not so serious. The truth was, I was scared as hell! What would they ask me? What would I have to do? Who would be there? What if I didn't really have an eating disorder and something was REALLY wrong with me? What if I didn't fit in?

As I bravely walked into the slightly darkened room, I was welcomed, seated, and went right into meditation. Um, what the heck is going on here? It was calm and peaceful, and I was the heaviest person in the room. That last part didn't really bother me as much as it surprised me. This debunked my first eating disorder myth: "Everyone with BED is overweight." Not true!

If you had taken all these women (eventually one man joined) to a mall, they in no way would stand out to you. No one would look at them and think they had eating issues. They looked just like you and me—normal. Whatever "normal" means.

Over the next seven months, I would make the 30-minute drive every Tuesday night to the two-hour class with anywhere from eight to ten people, mostly women.

We were given so many tools that I still use to this day and have tweaked to make my own. I learned about surfing the urge, mindful eating, how and why not to restrict, that I believed I wasn't important based on a childhood experience, and so much more ...

REFLECTIVE QUESTIONS

1. What did you learn about eating disorders in this chapter?
2. If a friend shared with you that they have an eating disorder, how would you respond?
3. What's your favorite food, and do you truly enjoy it when you eat it?

Chapter 17

THE HIDDEN STRUGGLE— UNDERSTANDING EATING DISORDERS

*E*ating disorders are a silent epidemic affecting millions of people around the world, yet they remain one of the most misunderstood and under-discussed mental health issues. While often associated with women, eating disorders also affect men, though the stigma and lack of awareness often keep their struggles in the shadows. In this chapter, we will explore the prevalence of eating disorders, the signs to look out for in yourself and others, and the importance of seeking help.

THE PREVALENCE OF EATING DISORDERS

Eating disorders are complex mental health conditions that involve an unhealthy relationship with food, body image, and weight. The most common types of eating disorders include anorexia nervosa, bulimia nervosa, binge eating disorder, and avoidant/restrictive food intake disorder (ARFID).

In the United States, 20 million women and 10 million men suffer from a clinically significant eating disorder at some time in their life, including anorexia nervosa, bulimia nervosa, binge eating disorder, or an eating disorder not otherwise specified.[4]

While these statistics are staggering, it's important to recognize that eating disorders don't discriminate—they affect individuals of all ages, genders, races, and socioeconomic backgrounds.

SIGNS TO LOOK FOR

Recognizing the signs of an eating disorder in yourself or others is crucial for early intervention and treatment. Eating disorders often start subtly, with changes in behavior and attitudes toward food, exercise, and body image. Here are some common signs to watch for:

1. Physical Signs:

- Noticeable weight fluctuations (either loss or gain)
- Frequent comments about feeling fat or gaining weight
- Preoccupation with food, calories, or dieting
- Avoidance of meals or situations involving food
- Dizziness, fainting, or fatigue
- Gastrointestinal complaints (constipation, bloating)
- Irregular menstrual cycles or amenorrhea (absence of menstruation) in women
- Hair thinning or loss, dry skin, brittle nails

---

[4] "What Are Eating Disorders?," NEDA, accessed September 29, 2024, https://www.nationaleatingdisorders.org/sites/default/files/ResourceHandouts/GeneralStatistics.pdf.

2. Behavioral Signs:

- Excessive exercise, often to compensate for eating
- Ritualistic eating behaviors, such as cutting food into small pieces or eating in secret
- Withdrawal from social activities, especially those involving food
- Evidence of binge eating, such as hoarding food or finding large quantities of food wrappers
- Signs of purging, such as frequent trips to the bathroom after meals, use of laxatives or diuretics, or the presence of vomiting
- Fixation on body image, including constant mirror checking or avoiding mirrors altogether

3. Psychological Signs:

- Intense fear of gaining weight or becoming fat, even when underweight
- Distorted body image, seeing oneself as overweight despite being underweight or at a healthy weight
- Depression, anxiety, or mood swings
- Low self-esteem or feelings of worthlessness
- Obsession with perfectionism and control

UNDERSTANDING THE SIGNS IN MEN

While eating disorders are often portrayed as a women's issue, men are equally vulnerable, though they may exhibit different signs and symptoms. Men with eating disorders may be more focused on muscle gain and achieving a lean, "ideal" physique, leading to a condition known as muscle dysmorphia. This can manifest as excessive weightlifting, extreme dieting to achieve low body fat, and the use of anabolic steroids or other performance-enhancing substances.

Men may also be less likely to seek help due to the stigma of having what is perceived as a "female" disorder. This can lead to under-reporting and a lack of treatment, making it even more important to recognize the signs and offer support.

THE IMPORTANCE OF SEEKING HELP

If you or someone you know is showing signs of an eating disorder, it's critical to seek help as soon as possible. Early intervention can make a significant difference in recovery outcomes. Treatment for eating disorders often involves a multidisciplinary approach, including therapy, nutritional counseling, and medical care.

> **Therapy:** Cognitive-behavioral therapy (CBT) is one of the most effective treatments for eating disorders. It helps individuals challenge and change distorted thoughts about food, body image, and self-worth. Other therapies, such as dialectical behavior therapy (DBT) and family-based therapy (FBT), may also be beneficial.

> **Nutritional Counseling:** Working with a registered dietitian who specializes in eating disorders can help

individuals develop a healthy relationship with food. Nutritional counseling focuses on restoring balanced eating patterns, addressing nutritional deficiencies, and educating individuals on the importance of nourishment.

Medical Care: Because eating disorders can have serious physical health consequences, medical care is often a critical component of treatment. Regular monitoring by a healthcare provider ensures that any medical complications are addressed promptly.

Eating disorders are serious mental health conditions that require compassion, understanding, and professional support. By recognizing the signs and seeking help, you can take the first step toward recovery and reclaiming your life. Remember, you are not alone, and help is available.

REFLECTIVE QUESTIONS

1. Have you noticed any changes in your eating habits, body image, or exercise routines that may indicate an unhealthy relationship with food?

2. Are there people in your life who may be struggling with an eating disorder, and how can you support them in seeking help?

3. What steps can you take to promote a healthy and positive relationship with food and body image for yourself and others?

RESOURCES

If you or someone you know is struggling with an eating disorder, there are resources available to help:

National Eating Disorders Association (NEDA): Offers support, resources, and treatment options. Visit nationaleatingdisorders.org or call their helpline at 1-800-931-2237.

The National Association of Anorexia Nervosa and Associated Disorders (ANAD): Provides free support groups, mentorship, and resources. Visit anad.org.

Eating Disorder Hope: Offers information on treatment options, support groups, and recovery resources. Visit eatingdisorderhope.com.

Chapter 18

THE BEAST REVEALED

*A*t 160 pounds, I was the heaviest one in the group. Most of us had binge eating disorder, and there was a woman who had anorexia nervosa. Some of the bingers also purged (bulimia), and there was a girl there who was a cutter.

This was the first time I had heard the term "cutter," and I eventually learned what that meant. To avoid feelings, she would cut herself with a sharp object where no one could see, and the pain from the cut is where her focus would go. Has this always been a thing, and I just never heard of it? Since then, I've discovered more and more people do it.

This is why we must talk about eating disorders, mental illness, cutting, and anything that gets put into the shame closet. When we talk about it, we can do something about it. Having an eating disorder felt lonely and isolating. Getting to be in a group and talking about it made it feel more real, and I was able to see I wasn't alone. In that, I was able to heal and feel "normal."

If you have an eating disorder or mental illness, I urge you to reach out to someone right now. Put down this book and ask for help—you are worth it!

Each eating disorder meeting would start with a meditation that was about five minutes long. I remember afterward, Dr. Bailey would ask, "How was that for you?" every single time. She would look so frustrated when each of us said, "Relaxing." I believe she was shooting for some major life-changing revelation that would expedite us into graduating from the program. Or at least that is what I told myself.

One day during meditation, about three months into my seven months of going weekly, I saw something. This was the turning point for me. With my eyes closed while hearing Dr. Bailey talk and guide us through the meditation, I saw a really big tree. This was the first time I saw something during our meditation. The tree wasn't even the big part; it was what was hiding behind the tree, and that was the breakthrough I was ready for and open to seeing.

If you've ever seen the movie *Harry and the Hendersons*, you know what I am talking about—Harry. The thing behind the tree was BIG, hairy, and was peeking out at me. Immediately, I knew this was my BEAST! The beast who would visit and appear as my friend and make me eat 10 times what I wanted to eat. The beast who made me feel inadequate. The beast that had taken over my life and stole so much joy from me over the years. That BEAST was my eating disorder.

When Dr. Bailey asked us to share, I gladly shared what I saw, and I believe even she was stunned by this sighting. Sharing this was uncomfortable for me. At the time, I was still quite shy and lacked confidence. The story I was telling myself was, "No one wants to hear what I have to say." Sharing my seeing "the Beast" came out of my mouth before I could second-guess myself and overthink whether they wanted to hear it or not.

Feeling insecure and lacking confidence is a huge part of an eating disorder, as well as body image. I never felt comfortable in my skin. So often, I wished I could just shrink right into the ground so no one could see or hear me. Sharing this crazy image that I saw was pivotal in my recovery.

As I shared, I battled inside what others were thinking of me and what I was saying. Do they believe me? Do they think I am making this up so that finally Dr. Bailey has an answer outside of "relaxing"?

As I described "the Beast" to the group, he became more and more lifelike in my mind, allowing me to identify with him and see his presence outside of me.

One day, I was out on my walk and could feel his presence, so I decided to talk to him. "Why are you here?" I asked. Although I don't remember his response, I do remember how powerful it was that I could talk to him, and if I could talk to him, that meant I could tell him to go away ... and I did! I told him, "I no longer need you, and there's no room for you in my life."

Yes, I realize this may sound crazy, and honestly, I don't care because it worked! Oh, he would come back from time to time to visit, and I would tell him the same thing, "You are no longer needed; go away."

Meeting my Beast was the biggest aha I had. During the seven months of weekly meetings, I also learned so much more.

At one meeting, we were introduced to A.I.B.s, or apparently irrelevant behavior. What the heck is she talking about ... oh, now I get it! An A.I.B. is when you buy some kind of food and/or bring it into the house for someone else.

My son likes these cookies, so I got them for him. Funny, that is a binge item for me.

There's a party this weekend so I will make a cake. Well, I might as well make two and keep one since we haven't had cake for a while.

My daughter has a class party this Friday, so I will make a treat for them and save some for myself.

Sound familiar? The apparent part in A.I.B. is the BS story you tell yourself. The relevant part is backing that BS story and making it seem as though you are selfless and doing this so kindly for someone else. Behavior is what you are doing so mindlessly. A trip to the grocery store or Costco gave me so many opportunities for A.I.B.s. Now, when I see and notice that trap, I laugh. "You're not going to get me this time!" I say to myself because out loud might make me seem crazy.

Having an eating disorder or anxiety, you have a lot of conversations in your head … it's very loud in there, and you really believe those stories. In one ED meeting, we were asked to review our stories with, "What evidence do you have?"

I believed that a family member didn't like me. It was a feeling I had, and if you asked me at the time, I may have said, "I feel it in my bones."

This, my friend, is EXACTLY what Dr. Bailey was talking about. What evidence did I have that this family member didn't like me? Did she come right out and say it? No. Did someone tell me she didn't like me? No. Did some super being come down and say she didn't like me? No. I had absolutely NO EVIDENCE to back up what I had been telling myself for YEARS! None. Zilch. Zero!

Here's the hard part: changing that story! Now what? I have believed for years this person does not like me based on some made-up story.

Well, now I get to wash away all that bull and be open for a new story, a story that better serves me.

The truth is, she's not very friendly, not only to me but to others. Oh my, you mean it's not about ME?!

That's another thing I learned from the ED group: we tend to think the world revolves around us. This comes across as a selfish act, and it is not because we are selfish or self-centered (or at least on purpose). It is because of this illness that robs you of having a full and complete life. Dr. Bailey suggested we look outside ourselves. Let me tell you, this is a practice and one that I continue to work on daily to this day!

Once you see how self-focused you are and get outside of yourself, you see the same trait in others. A word of advice: don't tell them. Yes, I speak from experience. This backfired on me. As we heal, we want to save the world. This is great AND is not always welcomed by others. If you see someone who is suffering, share your story. Do not tell them they need to do anything. Think how you would like someone to approach you if you were in their shoes. Be kind and gentle.

We did track our food, which was helpful because we had several categories. In addition to what we ate, we noted how we felt, whether we were hungry, where we ate, and whether we were mindful. We did not add the amount or caloric intake as this wasn't important. Dr. Bailey could see right through it if you were restricting. Restricting is what got us all into this mess in the first place.

Diet = restricting, PERIOD!

You can maintain restricting for so long before you snap, aka binge. So, no restricting. Having started dieting (restricting) when I was 12 and then 40, I knew two gears, restricting OR consuming—there was no in-between. This mind shift did not come easily for me or others.

The concept that there are no "good" or "bad" foods was very difficult to grasp. But, wait, I can eat cookies? I don't have to eat bland chicken breasts. What? I can have ice cream for lunch if I want? My mind was blown!

The next two days, I had ice cream for lunch! It was in my food diary, and as I handed it to Dr. Kashani for review, I held my breath and knew she was going to say something about it. The idea of my being "good" OR "bad" runs so deep, and when she didn't say anything about the ice cream, I didn't know how to react. This was new territory.

What I soon realized is that ice cream for lunch makes me cranky for the afternoon. Lesson learned! By the way, cookies do too.

The core of Dr. Bailey's program was mindfulness. Mindfulness has changed my life in all areas, not just food.

Eating mindfully, I realized I didn't like Pop-Tarts—they taste like cardboard. One of my favorite binge items was Kraft macaroni and cheese; eating it mindfully made me realize it was gross within the first bite! Eating mindfully opened up a whole new world (yes, I hear the music) of eating. Foods I thought I didn't like I discovered I do. I LOVE Brussels sprouts! Like, really love them! And broccoli and cauliflower. Eating mindfully made foods taste better and enhanced my eating experience. Food became fuel instead of the main focus—WHAT!?! After thinking about food 24/7 for YEARS, I would not think about it between meals because I wasn't restricting and ate foods that kept me satisfied.

From time to time, the temptation to restrict is there and I notice it. There's always an underlying reason. I am not moving my body enough, I feel like I am not producing the results I think I "should," or I ate something that still has the mental tag "bad." Mindful eating, like meditation, is a practice. Accepting there's no "good" or "bad" is a daily practice. Believing that I am neither "good" nor "bad" is a daily practice too.

The night I let Dr. Bailey know I felt like I was ready to graduate was met with excitement and sadness. After seven months, I had become an active and positive participant in the meetings. My place in the group added value and that made me feel proud.

My relationship with food is a million times better! There is still food noise (food that calls out to me from the pantry saying, "Eat me"), and I am better equipped to manage it. One residual occasionally trips me up, and that is when I am suddenly alone and think, "What can I eat?" If I'm hungry, I eat. If I'm not hungry, I don't.

REFLECTIVE QUESTIONS

1. What importance do you place on nutrition for your body's energy?

2. For your next meal, eat each bite mindfully and ask yourself, "Do I really like this food?"

3. When you were growing up, how did your family celebrate milestones?

Chapter 19

NOW THAT THE CAT WAS OUT OF THE BAG

*N*ow that my secret of binge eating was out to my husband and a few close friends (no one had any idea I was a binge eater), and I had therapy to move beyond it, the guilt and shame decreased. The interesting thing about that is now that binge eating didn't take up space in my head, there was a void, a void I wasn't sure how to fill. For over 25 years, I ate in secret and now can confidently eat all things out in the open.

That void, though ... how would I fill it?

One of my favorite pastimes is going up and down all the aisles at Costco. It calms me. Perhaps it's the high ceilings or all the merchandise. I'm not sure; it just makes me feel better. While going up and down all the aisles, I would find things I believed I needed and then put them into my cart. Crazy stuff like a three-pack of flashlights or a pack of 35 rolls of toilet paper. There was a strange comfort in having so much backup in my cabinets. "Just in case," I would tell myself. Buying in large quantities is liberating and exhilarating! It also paid off during the pandemic with a nice supply of TP!

My husband discovered he was allergic to fragrance, and we needed to use fragrance-free laundry detergent and fabric softener sheets, neither of which I could purchase at Costco in massive quantities. This was a huge disappointment, and I managed to get the necessary items at other stores.

In 2014, we did a major remodel in our house, including built-in cabinets in our hall. This created space for extra toilet paper, Kleenex, and paper towels. I even have one shelf dedicated to batteries, lots of batteries. You never know …

Then, along came Amazon, and simply hitting "Buy Now" became my favorite activity. The joy of seeing UPS driving up my driveway and dropping a beautiful brown box on my porch was like Christmas every day, only I was paying for it. Since Jens was away most of the time during the day at work, he didn't know how many boxes showed up at our door, and I was good at hiding the evidence before he came home. Old habits run deep.

That old familiar feeling of shame and guilt was back in my chest and jaw. It was comforting and horrible at the same time. With each purchase, I would say to myself, "This will be the last," or "No more for a week." I'd play games with myself and see how long I could go without making a purchase, and it wouldn't last more than a day or two.

In February 2016, while at a direct sales event, one of the directors mentioned going to a seminar and how it was life-changing for her. She was procrastinating every day and kept saying to herself, "Tomorrow will be better." After the seminar, she advanced very quickly in her business. It felt as though she was speaking directly to me as I sat in the front row at the edge of my seat.

Afterward, I went up to her to ask where she went. She said, "Klemmer & Associates." I immediately googled them and found out the next Personal Mastery (the first of four seminars they offer) was in Grand Junction, Colorado, in April, and I signed up, purchased a flight, and booked a hotel room.

This would begin a self-development journey that would completely change my life! Without giving away what goes on in the seminar room, I can say I got to challenge many beliefs about myself that were no longer serving me, let go of the anger I felt toward my mom, shift my "I can't" to "I can," and best of all, fill that void that was in myself with love for me. Real love, not the "fake it 'til you make it" love. For the first time in my life, I could say with complete and total honesty, I love myself! Success! That void is filled with love that only I could put there, no one else. Now I feel whole. Not just with words that Oprah or some mentor told me to say; I say them and know deep down in my core that I am worthy, I am beautiful, and I am whole.

When I was 48 years old, I finally discovered who I was, what I wanted, what I had to offer, and how valuable I was.

My son, in his seventh-grade year, made some horrible choices that got him suspended three times. The following summer, he went to Klemmer's Youth Leadership Camp and got to go deep and let go of his anger that he had been carrying for years which we didn't even realize he had or why he was so angry.

Looking back, I can clearly see how my upbringing and my mom's feelings about herself impacted me, and I can't help but wonder if Henry had inherited some of those same insecurities and traits. He and I share many similarities, both the positive and not-so-positive traits.

The time between April 2016 and May 2017 was what I call my transformation. I followed the saying, "Reinvent Yourself," with a new mindset, body, and career.

REFLECTIVE QUESTIONS

1. Have you reinvented yourself lately?
2. Who do you need to forgive today?
3. What's a new story you can tell yourself about your childhood?

Chapter 20

THE OSCARS, SORT OF . . .

*I*n December 2010, I retired from doing nails and took on a direct sales business in skincare and makeup, and I loved it! As a natural introvert, I learned how to get out of my shell, talk to others, and stand in front of a room and do training.

This direct sales company was designed to teach us confidence by getting up at our weekly meetings and sharing our successes for the week. There was a friendly competition, and you always cheered on other people as they grew their businesses too. It was a sisterhood like I had never experienced.

Because I loved the product so much, selling it was easy. I just shared it with everyone I knew, their friends, and their friends.

In my first year, I earned a beautiful diamond ring and got to walk on stage at the annual seminar to be recognized in front of thousands of women. It felt like the Oscars, and I was a movie star!

In the next year, I didn't work as hard and thought being on stage and earning a prize would "just happen." Well, it did not. At seminar that year, I did not earn a diamond ring, nor did I walk on stage. No fun at all!

The following year, I chose to work my business and was rewarded with an iPad since I didn't like any of the rings they offered as prizes and still got to walk on stage. Who would have ever thought, as a natural introvert, I would like the attention?

The next year, when I returned to the huge Oscars-like event, it was my best year ever!

When my category was called, they put me into the smaller group, the Top 20 group. Then, they sectioned me off and put me into the Top 10 group. As they called the names, starting with 10, they did not say my name. They kept calling out the names: 9, 8, 7, 6, 5, oh my goodness! My friends were there cheering me on and filming me (we affectionately called them "my film crew") as the person in fourth place was called, and now with the drum roll for the Top 3! I was the first runner-up and was given a super special sash. I felt like the queen! I was number 3 for sales in our seminar!

My love for leading and training others grew as I moved into directorship and led my own unit. My confidence grew and grew. What I loved most about my role as a director was coaching my team. I took a weekend workshop on how to lead and coach. Looking back, it was a total waste of money, so I won't mention the name. She read from a manual the whole time. Um, heck, I can do that! Wait, I CAN DO THAT! I realized I did have what it took to be a leader, train people in important areas, and get paid for it.

Insert Klemmer Coaching Academy.

One of the programs Klemmer offers is a coaching certification. It was one of my goals in my first Samurai Camp that is hosted by Klemmer.

REFLECTIVE QUESTIONS

1. What's one goal that could be life-changing if you went after it today?
2. What is one thing that would improve your life if you stopped doing it?
3. What is one thing that would improve your life if you started doing it?

Chapter 21

WHEN THE INTENTION IS CLEAR, A MECHANISM WILL APPEAR

*O*nce my binging was under control and my relationship with food normalized, I realized another issue: portion control.

The food I was eating was fueling my body and one may even say overfueling it. When I ate, I rarely felt full, and I could eat A LOT! I would eat each meal as mindfully as I could, tuning into my tummy. Sometimes I could feel the fullness, and sometimes I could not. This led to overeating.

In October 2016, at 195 pounds, I decided I was going to have weight loss surgery (WLS).

I knew that if my stomach were smaller, I could eat foods that fueled my body as I had been doing, just in smaller portions.

My mom had weight loss surgery over 20 years prior, and it was unsuccessful. She experienced weight loss immediately and then gained it all back and then some within a year or two of having the surgery. At the same time, a very close friend had the same surgery from the same surgeon and, to this day, has kept off the weight and lives a healthy lifestyle. I knew there was a chance of regaining. I also knew that it was my choice.

Through my Kaiser insurance, there is a process to be approved for WLS, and I was more than prepared.

First up, at 5′ 1.5″ and 195, my BMI was 35, and to get automatic approval, I needed to be at 40 or over 35 with health complications. The funny thing was that I was super healthy! My blood pressure was low, glucose tests were around 90, and I had no body pain or degeneration.

My doctor, Dr. Gonzales, had heard me talk about WLS for a few years and decided he would do all he could to get me the referral I needed to get into the surgeon.

Six years prior, I had some hip pain and had an x-ray. If an updated x-ray showed more deterioration, then that was my ticket. Dr. G jumped the gun and gave me the referral. The next hoop was an introduction class.

Introduction classes were once a month, and the next opening was in December, two months away. Nope, I was determined to get in sooner! I asked the guy if anyone cancels, and he said sometimes and to keep calling and checking. Later that afternoon, I called, and guess what? Someone canceled, and the next class was the following week! Success!

There was a tool that I learned in the self-development course that I used to expedite my surgery. When the intention is clear, a mechanism will appear, and the mechanisms kept appearing QUICKLY.

The next hoop was WLS orientation and meeting with the surgeon to get approval.

Here's where it got tricky. I knew I did not qualify for surgery by Kaiser standards and was determined that I would get it, so what did I do? I ate EVERYTHING! I did my absolute best to gain as much weight as possible—this is no easy task. Funny how when you are trying to lose weight, you gain, and when you are trying to gain, you lose.

I ate french fries every day.

The word on the street is it takes between four to six months from the first appointment to get the surgery, and when you are as determined as I was, that time gets cut drastically.

"It could take weeks or even months to get into the surgeon." That's what the lady said who led the introduction class. A week later, I got my appointment to meet with the surgeon the following week. This was going quickly! And I only had one week to gain 12 pounds. I ate more!

A major storm came in the morning of my appointment with the surgeon, dropping rain in sheets. The hospital where my appointment was being held was almost two hours away in morning Bay Area traffic and longer with the rain. Nothing was stopping me, nothing!

In the material I read, if you are late, don't bother because they will not take anyone late. When I arrived, I was 45 minutes late. The rain and traffic were worse than I thought! I persevered.

I walked into the orientation, which was already in session. The lady leading it asked if I was coming from Santa Rosa and that, with the rain and traffic, I was welcome to come in. What!?! My intention to get this surgery was so clear everything was falling into place!

When I arrived at Kaiser that morning, I did not pee and drank more water. When I got on that scale, I wanted to weigh as much as I possibly could. Words I never thought I would say. As I sat there listening to the leader, my bladder was screaming, and I ignored it. Finally, there was a break, and it was my turn to get on the scale. It read 204. It could have been my bladder, the french fries, the weights I put in my bra, or all the above, and I still wasn't at the 215 or more that I would need to be to get automatic approval. Panic!

After the orientation and using the restroom, I walked to the surgeon's office for my appointment. Dr. Layton is a man of few words, and the only word I was looking for that day was yes. He is the Chief of Bariatric Surgery at South San Francisco Kaiser.

As I waited in his office, I prayed. God, please let him say yes. I knew this was the answer for me, and I knew I was going to get good news that day.

Dr. Layton walked in, and my heart stopped. He is a lean, young-looking man who rarely looked me in the eye. He asked me questions about my years of dieting, how much I exercised, and about my general health and asked if he could see and touch my belly. Um, uh oh, remember, I have weights in my bra? Carefully, I lifted my top to reveal my belly. He pressed on it to check for scar tissue and said, "I believe you would do best with sleeve surgery." I looked at him with a blank stare. "Are you giving me approval?" I asked. "But I don't qualify; I'm not heavy enough."

His reply was, "Beckie, I know if I say no, you will be back here in six months after you have gained enough weight to qualify, so let's just take care of it now." I looked at him with tears in my eyes and said, "Thank you!" My instinct was to hug him, and if I wasn't worried about the weights falling out of my bra, I may have jumped up and hugged him. He knew I was happy. I knew I was happy. And I could go back to eating normally.

At that moment, I realized I had just been approved for weight loss surgery! Holy smokes!

It was now late October, only a couple of weeks after making the decision.

Next up were classes at Kaiser, lots of classes! For the record, I am grateful for every one of those classes because I learned how to be successful after WLS, what to expect before, during, and after WLS, and got a great deal of support.

By this time, my doctor got the x-ray back on my hip, and there had been no change in six years. This was great news, and the best part was I was already approved for WLS, so it didn't matter. Thank you, Dr. G!

Before you have WLS, you need to get a psychological evaluation to assess if you can undergo all the changes that are before you with this surgery. They are searching for stability, addiction, and any red flags that may prevent you from withstanding such a change in your life.

I can gladly say I passed with flying colors and was not surprised.

Since I had just returned from one of the seminars, I felt confident, full of myself, and excited about my future. The psychologist said he thought I was mentally in better shape than he was.

By this time, I had done so much work on my insides, overcome unworthiness, let go of the past, and loved who I was.

I set my sights on having the surgery in January, post-holidays. That made sense to me.

At one of my classes in mid-November, the lady instructing said everyone wants January, and if you are willing to go in December, you will have no problem getting in. Holy cow, that was only two weeks away!

That night, I went home and told my husband I would like to have the surgery in December. Truth be told, he was not on board with this whole surgery. He thought I could do it on my own and didn't think it was necessary. His biggest concern was how it would affect him and our life together. We loved eating and drinking, going out to nice dinners, and food. He is not a selfish man; he just couldn't see past where we were. I did.

The next day, I sent an email to my surgeon letting him know I wanted to be on the schedule for December and had lost the nine pounds he requested I lose before surgery. They usually request that you lose a certain amount of weight prior to surgery to show that you are serious. All I had to do was pee and remove the weights from my bra, and I was in.

On December 5, 2016, two months after making the decision, my husband drove me to South San Francisco Kaiser with no makeup and a small overnight bag to have the sleeve procedure done by Dr. Layton. That morning, I weighed in at 195, nine pounds lost right on the nose.

They say if you gain before surgery, they may cancel, and you will have to get back on the calendar.

I met two ladies in one of my classes, Julie and Allison. We were all scheduled for surgery the same day, and one right after the other went into the surgery room and under the knife.

When I was 15, I had my tonsils out. That was the only surgery I had ever had.

My husband waited the whole time. Although he wasn't for the surgery, he was for me, and I knew I had his full support.

When I woke up in recovery, I was in an enormous amount of pain, and they kindly gave me wonderful meds that took it all away. As I went in and out of consciousness, they took forever to get me a room. By then, Jens had driven home and would come to pick me up the next day.

The days following WLS felt like I did about 1,000 sit-ups, and I never took any pain meds. It was pretty easy, and since I had taken all of the classes at Kaiser, I knew exactly what to expect.

There are many bariatric support groups on Facebook, and any question I had was quickly answered.

At my two-week checkup, Dr. Layton said I could move from liquids to soft foods. Hallelujah!

After soft foods like scrambled eggs and cottage cheese, you graduate to foods like beans and soft meats. It is recommended never to have peas and corn because you don't really digest them, and they are a waste of space.

Common side effects after surgery are nausea and vomiting, sweating, constipation, hair loss, and diarrhea, which can occur after eating foods high in sugar. This is also called "dumping syndrome."

I did experience some hair loss at about three months post-op, although nothing noticeable. Other than that, I have been complication-free!

When I started my weight loss journey, I was in the "obese" category at 195 pounds. In the months that followed, I moved into the "overweight" category and then "normal" weight at 130. Actually, I am on the higher side of "normal" by medical standards at 130. The "normal" range for my height is 100-134. I prefer to go by how I feel in my clothes and how I see myself in my mirror. I do weigh myself every day as a guide, and do not let the numbers dictate my day. It's simply feedback on the gravitational pull of my body. I give it no energy anymore.

Given the choice, would I do it all over again? ABSOFRICKENLUTELY!!!

REFLECTIVE QUESTIONS

1. When did you feel your most confident?
2. What ritual, if any, do you have that gets you ready for a big event?
3. How do you cheer others on?

Chapter 22

THE DAY OUR WORLD CHANGED

$\mathcal{I}$t was Thursday, October 4, 2018. That day will be burned into my memory forever. It was the day that changed the direction of my son's life forever and mine too.

Mountain Academy, the prestigious private school my son was attending, called to let us know they suspected my son was selling weed to their students and that my husband and I needed to go to the school for a meeting ASAP.

That day, my husband just happened to be home from work, so we drove to Mountain Academy together. We were escorted into a room where my son was waiting with the Assistant Head of School, and later, the Head of School joined us. Henry looked petrified. I guess I did too.

As we sat there, I heard the dean and head of school say that selling drugs to students is a "line in the sand" and a reason for expulsion. EXPULSION, WHAT DID YOU SAY!?!

In between the time they called us and we arrived at the school, they confirmed that he had sold weed to a student.

In my mind, I thought this wasn't really happening. I wanted to crawl under the table and get into the fetal position. I could hear speaking, yet it was like a Charlie Brown cartoon, "Wamp, wamp, wamp."

As we sat there for what felt like hours, although it was probably only about 20 minutes, Henry was expelled from school. All I could think was, "At this moment, my 15-year-old son is not enrolled in school." I couldn't even process it.

The smorgasbord of emotions was shock, anger, stunned, pissed, embarrassed, ashamed, and uncertain of the future.

The head of school offered the name of someone who could guide us to the next steps. Next steps? Tomorrow, I will not be dropping him off at school here or any other school. Tomorrow, I will not be picking him up from school. Next steps? I'm not sure if I was breathing at that point, let alone deciding what to do with my son.

In all honesty, this did not come out of nowhere. In the months leading up to this day, I could see my son's behavior change. I knew he was doing weed and had been drinking some alcohol. What I didn't know was how much or how frequently. This would be revealed later, and it was staggering.

On the way home, I screamed, cried, and wondered what others would think and what would be next for our family.

Later that day, we met with a man named Robert Thomas. Bob, his preference, is a Therapeutic Placement Agent. A title I had never heard of before, mainly because I had never needed such a service.

Bob met with Jens and me first to get the situation down, then met with Henry privately and again with us. In his assessment, he suggested two roads to take. First, there was a local program for intensive outpatients encompassing weekly meetings for Henry, bi-weekly family meetings, weekly boys' meetings, and parent support group meetings every other week. In my gut, I knew this wasn't enough for Henry.

Insert the second choice, wilderness therapy. I had never heard of it before, and when we heard the price, we immediately discounted it. Holy smokes, $550 PER DAY!

The only thing we knew after that meeting was that something needed to change, and we needed Bob to help us get there. We just didn't know where "there" was yet.

This was all in one day, ONE FREAKING DAY. That night, when I got home, I poured myself the largest glass of wine possible. You know, to calm my nerves, gather my thoughts, get a grip on what just happened … and what's going to happen next.

The next day, I did not drop my son off at school because he wasn't enrolled. The shock had not worn off yet.

Henry went to the farm with Jens to make himself useful. What do you do with a kid who has been expelled? Ground him? Take away all his electronics? Send him off to military school? This was new territory, and no option felt like the right one; all the while, no option felt like the wrong one either.

That night, another BIG glass of wine to calm the nerves.

The big question was intensive outpatient OR wilderness therapy. As expensive as it was, I was seeing more and more of the benefits of wilderness therapy for Henry, and that night, when Jens caught Henry smoking weed in the garage, it was a no-brainer for me … wilderness therapy!

Even though, ultimately, this was a decision for Jens and me to make, we included Henry in some of the process. Interestingly enough, Henry didn't want the details; he wanted to be surprised … oh, that kid!

If you are not familiar with wilderness therapy, it's okay, I wasn't either. All across our states, several organizations offer various levels for our teens. The one we chose for Henry, Second Nature, is 24 hours a day, and seven days a week you are outside. You camp, eat, sleep, and, yes, poop outside. The skills kids learn are how to build a fire with a stick, twine, and some moss. They learn how bravado has played a role in their lives through movies, music, and seemingly innocent schoolyard talk. Their therapist works with them as individuals as well as a group.

The following Monday, Bob suggested the facility Second Nature Wilderness Therapy in Utah. My son would be flying to Utah for an undetermined amount of time, and we would not have regular contact with him.

Besides the name, cost, and where to issue that airplane ticket, we knew very little about what was happening and were still in shock over the whole thing.

On Wednesday, October 10, 2018, I put Henry on a plane with a one-way ticket to Salt Lake City, Utah, where on the other side two escorts would be meeting him. To this day, I still cry, more like bawl, recalling this memory. Because he was a minor, I got to walk him to the gate and see him walk down the tunnel.

As I watched him walk away, I said to myself, "How did we get here?"

Then I found a semi-secluded area, sat on the floor of the airport, and cried as hard as I could. At that moment, I couldn't care less about what people thought of me. My baby was gone, and I had no idea when I would see him again or what would become of him.

A side note here: For kids that do not want to go to wilderness therapy or don't know they are going, they will get a special treatment called "getting gooned," where two large men wake up the kid from a dead sleep and say, "Get up, we are going somewhere really fun." And before the kid knows it, they are swooped away on a plane and escorted the entire way.

Because Henry went willingly, he started off somewhat ahead of others, which would benefit him during his stay.

There it was; in less than one week since my son was expelled from school and sent away for God knows how long, I was navigating my way around this new way of life, if you can call it that.

I loved taking Henry to and from school and planned every day around it, knowing these days were limited. It is possible I used these drop-offs and pick-ups as an excuse to not get done all that I said I wanted to in a day and told myself I would get so much done while Henry was gone.

That was a lie, I told myself. Or maybe I told myself to fill my days with something instead of nothing.

During the 11 weeks Henry was at Second Nature, we got his letters every Wednesday and had a phone call with the therapist on Thursdays. After four weeks, Henry was able to join our calls. That first time I heard his voice after not hearing it for almost a month, I was so nervous. I was nervous talking to my own son! He was nervous too! It was awkward, and we muddled through it.

About four or five weeks into Henry's wilderness stay, I realized I was doing something I hadn't done in almost 10 years: binge eating. WHAT?!! I was about five days into it before I "came to" this realization. I believe I had gone into autopilot and was using a coping method deeply seated inside, and while in survival mode, it was my default. As soon as I realized it, I was able to course correct and get back on track thanks to all my tools.

On Wednesday, December 26, 2018, the day AFTER Christmas, we picked up Henry from a campsite in the middle of the Uinta Basin of Utah outside of Duchesne. We got to spend the day seeing and experiencing how he had lived for the last 11 weeks.

Life was slow, and the priority for the day was finding a good place to camp, build a fire, and cook. No Internet. No girls. No weed. No distractions. The kids there were just like Henry, good kids simply needing an opportunity to dig deeper and get the "stuff" out that had been haunting them.

We met the boys there and heard about their experience with Henry and what they hoped for him in the future. He was going home. That was not a common next step for kids at wilderness therapy. The next step typically is another therapeutic facility, like a boarding school. Henry was coming home with us, and I couldn't be happier and scared to death at the same time!

We got to sit in a circle with Henry, the boys, and the guides, and as they shared their experience of Henry and well wishes for his departure, it was clear that Henry had left his mark as a leader and an inspiration. One young man said the statistics of going straight home from wilderness successfully are low, and he knew Henry would beat the odds. That young man was right. When we got home, we all participated in family therapy, something we grew to enjoy, and I believe even our therapist liked us. He marveled at how openly we talked about ALL of our issues.

Although this time will go down in history as the most difficult I've ever experienced, it will also go down as the best investment ever! As I write this (over six years later), my son is doing remarkably well. He loves the young man he is and is excited about his future as he goes into his senior year at the University of Reno. I am enormously proud of him! Another reason it was a great investment is that a treatment center is tax-deductible. Who knew!?! We really needed the tax break that year.

If I had the choice again, I would do it over in a heartbeat!

REFLECTIVE QUESTIONS

1. If you could go back to your 15-year-old self, what advice would you give yourself?
2. What did you do in your younger years that has a hold on you and it's time to let it go?
3. What investment did you make in yourself that you believe was truly worth it?

Chapter 23

MY VICTORY MOMENT

*L*ittle did I know that while Henry was away, I would have the great opportunity to go to the Bahamas for a coaching conference, where I would have one of my biggest breakthroughs.

There I was, walking on the beach in the Bahamas in my swimsuit. It was a beautiful Sunday morning at SLS Baha Mar. I was there for a women's coaching conference, and during our stay, a famous football player got married at the hotel. One of the guests was Michael Jordan, the iconic basketball player I had wanted to meet for years. Fortunately, I got my wish. I got to meet, shake hands, and have a brief conversation with him. Seriously, it's one of the highlights of my life.

Back to the beach, my friend with whom I was rooming took an early morning flight home, and since my return flight didn't leave until later that day, I decided to park my bum on the beach. As I was sitting there, I decided I wanted to go for a stroll on this beautiful sandy beach. I got up and started walking. The sand felt glorious, and with each step, I felt my body feeling more and more relaxed.

Suddenly, I stopped right there in my tracks and gasped to myself. My body was exposed! No cover-up. No shorts or T-shirt. Just my body wearing a swimsuit on the beach for all the world to see. GASP! I looked down at my body, noticed my shadow, and thought holy cow, I have never walked a beach before without a cover-up. And then it hit me, I didn't freaking care! For the first time in my entire life, I walked on the beach in a bathing suit and didn't care how I looked or if my cellulite was showing. Not with an attitude of "I don't care," more like I love my body, and I am not letting ANYONE take that away from me. *Who am I*, I thought to myself?

I kept walking, and with every step, I believe I got a little taller and prouder, and I actually felt, dare I say, sexy in a swimsuit. Yes, I felt sexy! Pretty much my entire life, when I braved donning a swimsuit, I would cover up to walk the beach or use the restroom. Or I would put on shorts and a T-shirt to cover up. When I sat in the lounge chair or lay down on a towel, I would strategically place my legs, arms, and stomach in a way that I thought looked my best. So much time and energy went into looking just right.

Now, looking back on this effort, I wonder how many people noticed how I looked. Most likely, they were worried about how they looked and never even noticed me.

Since I was alone at the beach that day, and we live in an era of photo documentation, I took a selfie and then a photo of my shadow to mark this momentous day. Then, I did something that now makes me laugh so hard, like a full belly laugh. I looked up and around at the beach, only to see that I was the only one there. The previous version of me would have kept my head down, and in my mind, I would have thought everyone was staring at my cellulite and jiggly arms. This is the story I would have told myself, and then I see no one is even there. No one to shout out to, "I am wearing a swimsuit on the beach without a cover-up!"

My beach moment was in November 2018, and I still remember exactly how it felt. It felt like freedom. Freedom from what others thought of my body and freedom from worrying about covering up, hiding, and being obsessed with how I looked compared to others.

How many years, decades really, did I either avoid the beach or be so self-conscious that I couldn't be present with my friends and family with whom I was there? Photos that I didn't let others take. Or, if I let them take the photo, I would want to approve it or ask them to delete it. Well, back in the day, before digital cameras, I wanted to see the printed copy before anyone else.

REFLECTIVE QUESTIONS

1. What was your victory moment?
2. When do you feel your most confident?
3. What would you start doing if you had total body confidence?

Chapter 24

SHELTER IN PLACE URGES

*I*n March 2020, I was sitting on my couch in my house, and we were under a "Shelter in Place" order here in California due to the coronavirus. Stress levels were high, and the urge to stress eat sat on my shoulders. More than ever, I was aware of my coping mechanisms.

The urge to shop: stores are letting only so many in at a time, and the shelves are bare in a lot of areas. Online shopping looks about the same: "out of stock."

The urge to eat when I wasn't hungry was high, and I had given in to this urge a couple of times.

The urge to drink: earlier this year, I took a break from alcohol, and it changed my desire to drink and my habit of drinking daily.

So, how do I cope with unpleasant feelings now?

First up, I feel my feelings. If I'm feeling sad, scared, or angry, I recognize it instead of pushing it away. I am no longer scared of feeling unpleasant feelings because I know they will not last, and I am strong enough to experience them. The little girl in me has gotten stronger and braver. She no longer allows herself to feel shame or guilt, as much anyway. The grown woman I am now can fully step out of victim and into victor.

During shelter in place, I learned so much about myself as many of us did, as well as about human nature in general. There are three factors that make fear spiral out of control when things or life are unpredictable, uncontrollable, sustained, and chronic. The coronavirus was all three. We were being tested on all levels now. With those three factors in play, fear strikes hard! We like to know what is going to happen. We like to know, or at least believe, we can control things. We like to know when trouble will be over.

There is no better time to lean into what we can and can't control.

Whether you are a religious person or not, this prayer can be converted to fit your style:

> "God grant me the serenity
> To accept the things I cannot change;
> Courage to change the things I can;
> And wisdom to know the difference."

Surrender! I surrender.

Surrendering does not mean you are giving up! In fact, it is the opposite!

At a time like that, I chose surrender because I knew I could not control what was happening around me, only myself, my actions, and my choices.

At that time, and anytime, I know I am not perfect. I give in to urges and eat all the cookies or chips. The difference now, though, is that I don't beat myself up for it for days and weeks. The difference now is that the number on the scale no longer dictates whether I will have a good or bad day. I no longer see myself as "good" or "bad," I simply AM.

During shelter in place, I needed an outlet, like all of us, to work through the energy and difficulty I was experiencing. I would get in my car and drive around with the music on full blast and sing at the top of my lungs just to get the "guck" out. It was somewhat of a relief … and, I needed more.

REFLECTIVE QUESTIONS

1. How often do you give in to urges?
2. What would be different if you didn't give in to urges?
3. What would you like to do instead of giving into an urge? Think Plan B here … what would you like to do instead?

Chapter 25

FINDING YOUR TRIBE

*T*he people we surround ourselves with can significantly impact our self-esteem and well-being. Seek out people who lift and support you, rather than those who judge or criticize you based on your appearance. You deserve to be surrounded by positive influences encouraging you to be your best self.

Find your tribe! If, after walking away from a friend or family member, you always feel worse about yourself, they are NOT your tribe. Look at the people who are cheering you on over there on the sidelines. Those are your people.

People in your tribe shape your thoughts, emotions, and behaviors in ways you might not even realize. Therefore, it's crucial to be intentional about the relationships you nurture and the environments you immerse yourself in. Positive influences can elevate your spirits, support your growth, and help you become the best version of yourself. On the other hand, negative influences can drain your energy, reinforce your insecurities, and hold you back from reaching your potential.

In 2020, I had three close friendships dissolve, poof, gone. No conversation. No argument. No nothing, just done. I sat in my stuff over them for some time and then realized what I am sharing with you: finding your tribe sometimes means leaving the past.

That saying that some friends are in your life for a reason, season, or lifetime is so true!

FINDING YOUR TRIBE

One of the most important steps in cultivating a supportive environment is finding your tribe. Your tribe consists of people who genuinely care about you, celebrate your successes, and encourage you during challenging times. They are the ones who lift you up and inspire you to be your best self. If you constantly feel worse about yourself after interacting with a particular friend or family member, it may be time to reevaluate those relationships. Those who criticize, judge, or belittle you are not your tribe.

RECOGNIZING TOXIC RELATIONSHIPS

Recognizing toxic relationships is the first step in distancing yourself from negative influences. Toxic relationships often leave you feeling drained, anxious, or demoralized. These individuals might be highly critical, unsupportive, or manipulative. They may undermine your confidence and make you question your worth. Here are some signs that a relationship might be toxic:

- **Constant or Subtle Criticism:** Instead of offering constructive feedback, toxic individuals frequently criticize and belittle you.

- **Lack of Support:** They show little interest in your achievements and may even downplay your successes.

- **Manipulation:** They manipulate your emotions to control you or get their way.

- **Jealousy:** They feel threatened by your accomplishments and may try to sabotage your efforts.

- **Negativity:** They have a pessimistic outlook on life and often focus on the negative aspects of any situation.

CULTIVATING POSITIVE RELATIONSHIPS

Once you've identified toxic influences, it's essential to seek out and cultivate positive relationships. These are the people who cheer you on from the sidelines, offering genuine support and encouragement. They listen without judgment, provide constructive feedback, and celebrate your victories, no matter how small. Surrounding yourself with positive influences can significantly enhance your self-esteem and overall well-being. Here are some ways to cultivate positive relationships:

Identify Your Supporters: Take a moment to reflect on the people in your life who consistently support and uplift you. These individuals are your true supporters. They may be friends, family members, colleagues, or mentors. Make an effort to spend more time with them and nurture these relationships.

Communicate Openly: Open and honest communication is the foundation of any healthy relationship. Share your thoughts, feelings, and goals with your supporters. Let them know how much you appreciate their presence in your life. Likewise, be a good listener and offer your support in return.

Set Boundaries: Establishing healthy boundaries is crucial in maintaining positive relationships. Boundaries help protect your emotional well-being and prevent others from overstepping. Clearly communicate your boundaries and be firm in upholding them. It's okay to say no to things that drain your energy or compromise your values.

Engage in Shared Activities: Spend quality time with your tribe by engaging in activities you all enjoy. Whether it's hiking, cooking, or attending events together, shared experiences can strengthen your bond and create lasting memories.

Seek Out New Connections: Don't be afraid to expand your social circle, and seek out new connections. Join clubs, organizations, or online communities that align with your interests and values. Meeting new people can introduce fresh perspectives and enrich your life.

THE POWER OF POSITIVE INFLUENCES

Surrounding yourself with positive influences can have a transformative effect on your life. Here are some ways in which positive relationships can enhance your well-being:

Boosting Self-Esteem: Positive influences help you see your strengths and potential. They celebrate your accomplishments and remind you of your worth. This boost in self-esteem can empower you to pursue your goals with confidence.

Encouraging Growth: Positive relationships provide a safe space for personal growth. Your supporters encourage you to step out of your comfort zone, take risks, and embrace new challenges. They believe in your potential and push you to reach higher; in turn, you do the same for them.

Providing Emotional Support: Life is full of ups and downs, and having a strong support system can make all the difference. Positive influences offer a listening ear, a shoulder to cry on, and words of encouragement during difficult times. They help you navigate challenges with resilience and grace.

Fostering a Positive Mindset: Being around positive people can inspire you to adopt a more optimistic outlook on life. Their positivity can be contagious, helping you focus on the good in any situation and maintain a hopeful attitude.

Enhancing Overall Well-Being: Positive relationships contribute to belonging and connection. They fulfill your basic human need for companionship and social interaction. This sense of community can enhance your overall well-being and happiness.

By intentionally surrounding yourself with positive influences and creating a nurturing environment, you can enhance your self-esteem, foster personal growth, and achieve a greater sense of well-being. Remember, you deserve to be surrounded by people who encourage and support you, helping you become the best version of yourself. Find your tribe, set healthy boundaries, and cultivate relationships that lift you up and inspire you to thrive.

REFLECTIVE QUESTIONS

1. Who are the people in your life who consistently uplift and support you, and how can you nurture these positive relationships further?

2. Reflect on a recent interaction that left you feeling drained or demoralized. What boundaries can you set to protect yourself from negative influences?

3. How can you create a positive environment that supports your well-being and aligns with your values?

Chapter 26

CULTIVATING GRATITUDE

"*C*omparison steals, gratitude heals." That quote came to me while in the shower one day. Gratitude is the miracle cure. Right now, take a moment to look around you and find three things you are grateful for. Now, look at your body and find three things you are grateful for.

Searching for something to be grateful for on your body if you can't find anything ... what about your pinkie toe, do you like that? Your smile, eyes, or wrists?

There's a saying I have, "You always find what you are looking for." If you're looking for flaws and cellulite, you will find them every single time. If you are looking for the beauty in your body, you will find it! When you do, fill up with gratitude.

Every single night before I go to sleep, I write down 10 things for which I am grateful. Some are as simple as a delicious cup of coffee. Or I go a bit deeper thinking about a new client or a smooth-driving shopping cart. Finding something to be grateful for at the end of the day for five-plus years now has opened up my daytime awareness of noticing all of the "good things."

When I get a green light, I whisper, "Thank you." When another driver lets me into the lane, I wave and whisper, "Thank you." When something plays out in my favor, I whisper, "Thank you." Being in a constant state of gratitude attracts more gratitude.

Recently, I was walking into a store, and a young girl, around eight, was walking out with her dad. She was sporting a brand-new backpack. She spun around and had a look of pure joy on her face. I paused, noticed, and then felt grateful that I got to witness that blessing. It was like Christmas day for her, and she just got a new puppy. That was a gift to witness.

Practice gratitude every single day.

In my Body Confidence Program, I have my clients ask what qualities their friends and family see in them. That conversation would sound something like: "Hi, Beth, I am doing a program, and I get to ask my friends and family what qualities they see in me. Would you be willing to share with me?"

Some get excited, and others push back. Either way, it's a highly effective experience to see what others see in you so you can discover more reasons to be grateful for yourself and your body.

One of my clients who went through the Body Confidence Program a second time confessed to not asking anyone the first time around. Through some coaching, she decided to take on this assignment. The next week, she couldn't wait to share all the kind and enlightening things that her friends and family had to say about her. She beamed!

You know where this is going … ask your friends and family what qualities they see in you, and write them down. Please don't text or email this question. Ask in person or over the phone. After they share with you, offer them the same gift by sharing the qualities you see in them.

If you struggled to find something about yourself to be grateful for, now you have qualities your friends shared. This is the soil to grow your gratitude.

Have you ever heard of a "Brag Book?" To some, the word "brag" may bring up a negative meaning. I get it; I did too. Hear me out. A client of mine said she wanted to be more spiritual, yet she wasn't clear on what that meant to her and how she wanted that to look. Through coaching, she discovered that she lacked confidence in herself and in most areas of her life. She was very successful in her career, in great shape, ate healthy, and was in a loving marriage. She had an unfavorable event occur at work. She was falsely accused of doing something, and even though it was corrected, she allowed it to take the wind out of her sails. She needed something to fill her up. Enter "Brag Book."

She got a notebook, and, in the front of it, wrote down positive things she saw in herself. In the back, she wrote what others said about her. To see her confidence grow over the eight weeks was inspiring. She went from being unsure of herself to standing tall and confident all because of this book of gratitude for herself. That, my friend, is the power of gratitude.

I invite you to start your version of a brag book if you want to increase your confidence or gratitude for yourself. If the word "brag" doesn't ring with you, use "Things I Like About Me," "Evidence I Am Worthy," or "This Is Me" as the title to the book about all of your awesomeness. Once you start looking for all the reasons you are incredible, you'll find more and more and start seeing what was there all along and what others see.

Being and feeling gratitude about yourself is not arrogant or egotistical. It's self-love. It's also a way to set boundaries. Yes, boundaries. Seeing the good in yourself builds up your confidence, and in that confidence, you grow stronger. In that strength, you are better equipped to stand up for yourself and stop allowing others to tear you down or take advantage of you. So brag on about your bad self! I am over here cheering you on!

A fun and transformative tool to elevate your gratitude practice is something I like to call "The Most Magnificent Award." This simple yet powerful exercise encourages you to actively seek out and acknowledge the extraordinary in your everyday life. Start by looking around and identifying moments, objects, or people that stand out for their beauty, joy, or significance.

For instance, notice the most magnificent rose on the bush; its vibrant colors and perfect petals are a testament to nature's artistry. Or savor the most magnificent meal you've just eaten, appreciating the flavors, textures, and love that went into its preparation. Maybe it's the most magnificent smile you've ever seen on a human, a genuine expression that lights up their entire face and warms your heart.

When you find these moments of magnificence, mentally bestow them with "The Most Magnificent Award." You can do this verbally, sharing your appreciation with others, or simply acknowledging it within yourself, taking a mental note of the award. By doing this, you train your mind to focus on the positive and extraordinary aspects of your daily experiences, enhancing your sense of gratitude and wonder. This practice uplifts your spirit and creates a ripple effect of positivity as you begin to see and celebrate the magnificence all around you.

Over time, this exercise can shift your perspective, helping you to recognize and appreciate the beauty and joy that might otherwise go unnoticed. It's a playful and engaging way to deepen your gratitude practice, making it a regular part of your life and fostering a more appreciative and content mindset. So, go ahead and start awarding the magnificence in your life, and watch as your sense of gratitude and happiness flourishes.

REFLECTIVE QUESTIONS

1. What are some things in your life that you take for granted?
2. How has practicing gratitude affected your mood and outlook on life?
3. How can you incorporate gratitude into your daily routine?

Chapter 27

MY IMAGE NEMESIS

$\mathcal{S}$etting goals that are meaningful to you can help you focus on what really matters in your life. Consider what you want to achieve in your career, relationships, and personal growth. When you focus on these areas, you'll start to realize that your physical appearance is just **one** small part of your overall happiness and success.

Enter Image Nemesis—what you are willing to do versus what you want to do.

A lot of people ask me how I went from loathing to loving my body after not losing a pound. Two words: Image Nemesis.

You may think, hmmm, I've never heard of Image Nemesis before and may want to google it. There's a reason you have not heard of it because it's my creation, brainchild, or coined phrase. Whatever you want to call it, it's mine, and I used it to have an epiphany of how I saw and felt about my body.

One day, I was driving and had this revelation about how I saw my body versus how I thought my body "should" look. I say should because I was able to pull out an image that I unconsciously had been carrying in my mind about how I thought I should look, and that if I did look this way, my life would be PERFECT!

You see, even though I am a petite woman, I have large bones per my wrist measurement and tend to carry more fat than muscle.

My epiphany came with an image of a toned, hard body woman that I unconsciously held, believing that if I looked like her, I would be smarter, more confident, always know what to do in every situation, and that all men would want me and women would want to be me.

Having this awareness was groundbreaking for me. I had no idea I was always comparing myself to this image. I didn't consciously realize that every time I started a diet or a workout routine that deep in my subconscious, I secretly wanted to look like that image, and if I didn't, I saw myself as unsuccessful, fat, and an all-out loser. This all went on behind the scenes and outside of my every-day awareness. It was as if my body/mind was working against itself, and I would never win, EVER!

It's like those games at the fair that are rigged, so you can't win. That was me—the Coke bottle with a pole and a string, and no chance of picking up the bottle and getting the prize.

I would lose every time because I didn't know the game I was playing, nor was I aware of the rules I had unconsciously created.

To say this was huge is a total understatement!

The program that I created based on this epiphany, The Body Confidence Method, has had many members discover their Image Nemesis and recognize the game they, too, had been playing where they would never win ... it's been a game changer for me and many others. It's my hope that you too discover your Image Nemesis so you can recognize it for what it is, an image created by your subconscious.

Now that I have come to this realization, what's next?

This is where it really gets juicy. I was able to shift from this hard body image to a realistic version of my most excellent self.

My most excellent self is who and what I am willing to do. The key word there is *willing*.

I created an image in my mind of the real me on one side and my Image Nemesis on the other and then thought about all the things between us. What would it take for me to actually look like that hard body?

I would have to work out six days a week for several hours, eat mainly chicken breasts, no candy or drinking wine, and be disciplined 100% of the time. WOW, this come to Jesus moment was a tough one. Was I willing to do all of this? No. Actually, it was more of a heck no! I know myself. Perhaps I could do that for a while, yet I could not maintain this long-term.

I call everything between my Image Nemesis and me "The Gap."

Why was this such a huge revelation? Again, every time I started a health journey, this image, which I had no conscious awareness of, was in the back of my mind, and I was never going to be able to achieve it by what I was doing, so I unknowingly set myself up to fail EVERY SINGLE TIME!

What I did with this information created a reinvention of myself. There was one question I asked myself that changed it all for me.

What am I willing to do?

Willing. That was the word that changed my image of myself. Once I asked what I was willing to do, I knew I was not willing to do everything I needed to become that hard body. I let that Image Nemesis go. Poof, gone!

She did go away … and she comes back to visit from time to time. The difference is that now I recognize her and can go back to choosing the image that I am creating, which is a realistic and excellent version of myself. The one I am willing to create.

I am willing to stretch myself to be better from a place of honoring my body along with all it does for me and love any imperfections there too, while releasing that perfect hard body.

Women who have gone through my program found their Image Nemesis in a younger version of themselves, a taller or shorter version of themselves, or that time they lost all that weight and felt so good.

When your Image Nemesis is the last example, that time you lost all that weight, think back: did you truly appreciate your body? Did you love and accept it? Or is that how you feel now reflecting on it?

I love it when I see a photo of myself, and think, "Wow, I wish I was as fat as I felt I was in that photo," where I was 20 pounds lighter and yet felt fat at the time.

REFLECTIVE QUESTIONS

1. What is your Image Nemesis?
2. What is in your gap?
3. What are you willing to do?

Chapter 28

GETTING YOUR MOJO BACK

I f my problems didn't lie in my thighs, then where did they lie? In my head!

Years ago, I had a client, Dana, who was an Olympic athlete on top of her game. Then, long after the medals, attention, and rigorous training, she stopped working out, gained weight, and lost herself in a new lifestyle that in no way resembled discipline and structure. Who was she now? This is a question Dana asked herself for years.

Coming from a place of popularity and status-driven to weight gain and living a humble life, she was embarrassed and wanted to hide. As I sit here with an extra 10 pounds, I can relate.

Seasons in our lives bring about change, which isn't always fun or comfortable. In Dana's case, without the intense and rigorous coaching and daily drive, she didn't know how to exist. When she came to me, she shared that she felt like a failure and didn't know how to get out of this phase.

This "phase" happens to most of us in the form of pregnancy, injury, menopause, or massive life transitions. Of maybe even all of the above.

Maybe you've never been an Olympic athlete, and neither have I. However, the message is still the same: we can get through this season and come out better if we choose to. Yes, there will be another season ... and another ...

Self-sabotage has a way of finding itself in my life, and recently, I had a huge aha around how I was wreaking havoc on my physical life. In 2023, I trained for an event called 29029 Everesting, where you hike the equivalent of Mt. Everest at a ski resort that they rent for the weekend. You have 36 hours to complete, and my venue was Sun Valley, Idaho, where you would ascend the mountain 15 times to reach a total gain of 29,029 feet of elevation. If you completed it, you would earn a red hat. As a person who loves shiny objects, I was won over by earning a red hat, which drove me to train and keep climbing up that mountain.

I earned my red hat in 28 hours and, with that, also earned the title of "Endurance Athlete." Wow, from a girl who got picked last to be a player in school sports to an Endurance Athlete, that was pretty cool. Then I went on to run my first half marathon and earned a cowbell—that was cool too!

Then I took a rest. I told myself it would just be during the holidays, then I would get back to training. This is temporary, right? Valentine's Day counts as a holiday, right? St. Patrick's Day, Easter, Fourth of July ... okay, now the season is more than a season; it's a lifestyle, and it doesn't serve me. How do I shift out of this?

Remember that learn to run course, "Couch to 5k"? As I write this, that's how I feel. Have you ever gone so hard and pulled back the throttle only to realize there's no gas in the tank, and the spark isn't there? Yeah, me too.

This is what I call losing my mojo, cue Austin Powers.

How do I get my mojo back? Have you lost your mojo and want to get it back? Maybe you never had your mojo and want to find it … let's go!

First, there will be setbacks, and if you know this from the start, you can better prepare and be ready to move through them. Have you ever heard the term "New level, new devil"? Well, it's pretty much a guarantee that when you choose to take on something new and big, there will be roadblocks along the way. Please know I don't share this to be negative or put that in your mind; I share it because it's real and happens. As you start to find your mojo you could get sick, have an injury, or suddenly a parent may need your help. It happens, and it will always happen. Now that you know, you won't be surprised. I find being surprised can be yet another setback that can take some time to get over.

My first step is simply noticing that I have lost my mojo. To me, this feels like low energy and a lack of motivation, and my drive is pretty much gone. Others have described it as no direction, feeling lost, or being non-empathetic. You may have a different description, and I would love to hear it. Share it with me on my Instagram page @BeckieKullberg.

My second step is to give myself some grace. Maybe I need to take a break or get some rest. Then I focus on gratitude and the things that bring me joy. Nature is one of the quickest ways to get grounded and rejuvenated. Find the things that bring you joy, and do them as often as possible.

REFLECTIVE QUESTIONS

1. What transition did you go through that shifted your overall confidence?

2. How did you weather it?

3. Who do you know that had the same experience, and how did they overcome it?

Chapter 29

WHAT'S NEXT . . .

*Y*ou may be asking, how did that 15-year-old girl heal from the thigh comment during sex, or the 21-year-old young woman from the verbally abusive relationship, from an eating disorder and a husband who left me for another woman, and more? The answer isn't an easy or short one; it's complicated and a bit messy.

I could say I've given myself grace, forgiven myself for my choices, or had some epiphany around it all and suddenly came into a place of euphoria. If I said that, I would be lying and selling myself short.

The way I see it, all of my stuff made me into who I am today, and my today person with all of her scars, scrapes, and bruises is pretty freaking awesome!

Setbacks used to take me out for days, weeks, and sometimes even months. Now, I am quick to dust myself off and keep going. That resiliency comes from falling and getting back up over and over again. That bounce-back ability is my superpower and one I wear proudly.

When I stopped chasing the notion that I need to make all of this make sense or have some big sign hit me in the face while asking God, "Why me?" I accepted that this is me! Again, with the *Greatest Showman*. This is me, and I am damn proud of myself!

Overcoming adversity doesn't have to be complicated or drawn out unless you like that sort of thing. It can simply be taking a deep breath and saying, "I got this." Also, "I forgive myself." Because I have no control over others, taking ownership of my actions and choices has been a huge needle-moving process.

There's no such thing as overnight success. Instead, it's a series of incremental small successes that one day, when you look back, you see an enormous amount of progress, forgiveness, grace, self-love, and self-confidence.

I wrote the bulk of this book in 2020 before I started hiking and growing even more self-confidence, and I was so scared to think of my husband, my son, my 97-year-old mother-in-law, my friends, and total strangers reading all of this about me that I put it away.

Then, I started writing an entirely different book about facts and statistics on why our problems don't lie in our thighs. I realized that it needed a personal story; it needed my story. My story of overcoming an eating disorder, anxiety, poor self-esteem, and body confidence issues wasn't quite complete yet.

My "New level, new devil" is Imposter Syndrome, and I'm nipping at her heels and just about to pass her. She's a killer of souls, and she's not taking mine!

The journey to get where I am now has been one bumpy ride, and it's not over! Prior to my son going into Wilderness, the most difficult thing I'd ever experienced was my second husband leaving me for another woman. I seriously hope the Wilderness experience will be the last and most difficult one. However, I know I am better equipped to overcome adversity than before the experience. I choose to get stronger, be more resilient, and break through beliefs that hold me back. I am a BADASS, and I love myself! The best part is I can write that without worrying "Oh gosh, what will others think of me?"

I learned that others will think what they think and guess what? I have no freaking control over it! That, my friend, is so empowering! Are there things in this book that no one has ever known? Yes, and that scares the shit out of me!

When the time comes for my husband to read this, he may see me differently. However, I know he will still love, respect, and support me, which gives me the courage to share my story.

Over my 57 years on this earth, the constant that I have learned is that things will change, life will change, and with every adversity, I get stronger, and so will you. Most importantly, the problems do not lie in your thighs, and they never did; they are in your head, and only you can overcome them.

You have a story, we all do, and I encourage you to share it. You don't need to write a book if you don't want to … share it with someone; you never know who you will inspire.

My son is one of the most courageous people I know! When he returned from Wilderness, he proudly shared his experience. I personally grew as I watched him bravely take on his new life post-Mountain Academy and start a new school mid-year. My son gives me the courage to be and do better because I want him to be proud of me.

My husband has been one of my biggest supporters. He can let things just roll right off of him and never holds a grudge. I am grateful for him every single day.

In my space now, I stand taller and feel enormous pride for myself. Am I where I want to be, or thought I would be at 57? When I surrender and accept where I am, I feel lighter, and the pressure to be "perfect" fades. The urge to compare myself to others at my age, or even younger, slightly dissipates.

Comparison is death to happiness.

My journey continues, and I say, "Bring it on!"

REFLECTIVE QUESTIONS

1. What's next for you?
2. What are you most excited about for your next chapter?
3. Who will you share this book with?

WATCH YOUR LANGUAGE

*T*he way we talk to ourselves shapes our reality. Have you ever read *The Secret?* Our internal dialogue can be a powerful tool for growth and self-empowerment or a destructive force that holds us back. Many of us use demeaning or insulting language without even realizing it. This chapter, "Watch Your Language," aims to bring awareness to your self-talk and provide strategies to transform it into a supportive and empowering dialogue.

THE POWER OF WORDS

Our words carry weight, and if you're looking to lose weight, here you go. The language we use with ourselves can either uplift or diminish our sense of self-worth. Phrases like "I should," "I can't," or "I'll try" subtly undermine our confidence and resolve. By becoming conscious of these phrases and actively replacing them with more empowering alternatives, we can foster a healthier self-image and greater self-efficacy.

Many words and phrases you use may seem benign or perfectly harmless, and yet your subconscious is listening. Just like Alexa, your subconscious is ALWAYS listening and taking everything literally.

I've heard people say to themselves, "I tell my fat ass to get going," "My butt is so big ..." or "I'd be a whole lot happier if I just lost weight."

The message that is going directly to your subconscious is, "I'm fat," "my butt is big," and "I am sad."

COMMON DEMEANING PHRASES AND THEIR ALTERNATIVES

"I should" vs. "I can": "Should" implies obligation and can lead to feelings of guilt and inadequacy. Replacing "I should" with "I can" shifts the perspective to one of capability and choice. For example, instead of saying, "I should exercise more," say, "I can choose to exercise for my health."

"I can't" vs. "I will": "Can't" is a definitive statement of incapability. Replacing it with "I will" transforms it into a declaration of intention and commitment. For instance, instead of saying, "I can't finish this project," say, "I will focus and complete this project step by step."

"I'll try" vs. "I will" or "I won't": "Try" often carries a built-in excuse for failure. Committing to either "I will" or "I won't" removes ambiguity and sets clear intentions. For example, instead of saying, "I'll try to be more organized," say, "I will implement a new organization system."

STEPS TO TRANSFORM YOUR SELF-TALK

Notice Without Judgment: The first step is awareness. Pay attention to your self-talk without judging yourself for it. Simply observe the phrases and words you use regularly. Keep a journal to record instances of negative or demeaning self-talk.

Reframe Your Language: Once you're aware of your self-talk patterns, begin to reframe them. Replace negative phrases with positive alternatives. Practice this consistently until it becomes a natural habit. For example, if you catch yourself thinking, "I'm terrible at this," reframe it to, "I'm learning and improving every day."

Practice Self-Compassion: Treat yourself with the same kindness and compassion you would offer a loved one. Ask yourself, "Would I speak to a friend or family member this way?" If the answer is no, it's time to change the way you talk to yourself. Practice self-compassion by acknowledging your efforts and celebrating your progress, no matter how small.

Set Clear Intentions: Use clear and affirmative language to set your intentions. Instead of vague or uncertain statements, be specific and assertive about your goals and actions. This clarity reinforces your commitment and boosts your confidence.

Create Affirmations: Develop positive affirmations that resonate with you and repeat them daily. Affirmations like "I am capable," "I am worthy," and "I am growing" can help reinforce positive self-talk and build a stronger, more supportive inner dialogue.

By watching your language and transforming your self-talk, you can cultivate a more positive and empowering mindset. This shift not only enhances your self-esteem but also propels you toward achieving your goals with greater confidence and clarity. Remember, the problem does not lie in your thighs or any other part of your body; it often lies in the words you choose to speak to yourself.

REFLECTIVE QUESTIONS

1. What common negative phrases or words do you use when talking to yourself, and how can you reframe them into positive alternatives?

2. How does your current self-talk compare to the way you speak to your loved ones? What changes can you make to treat yourself with the same kindness and compassion?

3. Reflect on a recent situation where you used negative self-talk. How could you have reframed your language to be more supportive and empowering?

CONCLUSION

*I*t's time to stop believing that the problem lies in your thighs, or any other body part for that matter. Your physical appearance does not define your worth or your ability to be happy and successful. By shifting your focus away from your appearance and toward what really matters in your life, you can start living a more fulfilling, balanced life. Practice self-care, gratitude, and self-compassion, surround yourself with positive influences, and focus on finding joy beyond your appearance. When you do this, you'll be able to break free from the myth of physical perfection and create a life that truly makes you happy.

Instead of judging or resisting the person who made less-than-desirable choices, send her love. Send her grace. Send her a thank you! Thank you for doing all of the things that you did to get me to where I am today, and I love the me I see in the mirror.

To see what I am up to now, visit me at beckiekullberg.com, and find me on social media, and tag me in a post of you reading this book.

ABOUT THE AUTHOR

*B*eckie Kullberg is a Certified High-Performance Coach dedicated to helping individuals transform their lives by embracing self-love, empowerment, and personal growth. With a passion for guiding women through their own journeys of healing and confidence, Beckie shares her personal experiences and insights to inspire others to overcome body image struggles and reclaim their worth.

Living in beautiful Sonoma County, Beckie is an avid hiker who finds peace and strength in nature. She brings the same passion and resilience to her coaching, helping clients achieve their goals and live with purpose. As a coach on the Aura Health app, she provides mindfulness and wellness practices to thousands of listeners, empowering them to see life from a new and refreshing perspective.

Through her work, Beckie combines her personal healing journey with her professional expertise, offering women all over the world the tools they need to live empowered, confident lives. *The Problems Do Not Lie in Your Thighs* is a reflection of her deep commitment to guiding others toward self-acceptance and fulfillment.